ASHE Higher Education Report: Volume 30, Number 6
Adrianna J. Kezar, Kelly Ward, Lisa Wolf-Wendel, Series Editors

Beyond Grade Inflation

Grading Problems in Higher Education

Shouping Hu

Beyond Grade Inflation: Grading Problems in Higher Education
Shouping Hu
ASHE Higher Education Report: Volume 30, Number 6
Adrianna J. Kezar, Kelly Ward, Lisa Wolf-Wendel, Series Editors

ISSN 1551-6970   electronic ISSN 1554-6306   ISBN 0-7879-8078-1

The ASHE Higher Education Report is part of the Jossey-Bass Higher and Adult
Education Series and is published six times a year by Wiley Subscription Services,
Inc., A Wiley Company, at Jossey-Bass, 989 Market Street, San Francisco, Califor-
nia 94103-1741.

For subscription information, see the Back Issue/Subscription Order Form
in the back of this journal.

CALL FOR PROPOSALS: Prospective authors are strongly encouraged to contact
Kelly Ward (kaward@wsu.edu) or Lisa Wolf-Wendel (lwolf@ku.edu). See "About
the ASHE Higher Education Report Series" in the back of this volume.

Visit the Jossey-Bass Web site at **www.josseybass.com.**

Printed in the United States of America on acid-free recycled paper.

Advisory Board

The ASHE Higher Education Report Series is sponsored by the Association for the Study of Higher Education (ASHE), which provides an editorial advisory board of ASHE members.

Contents

Executive Summary

The general public has become less confident about grading practices in higher education in a time when many reports on grade inflation appear frequently in the news (Arenson, 2004; Healy, 2001). As calls for accountability of student learning intensify, colleges and universities need to reexamine their grading practices and restore public confidence in college grades.

Student learning is one of the central functions of undergraduate education. Grades, despite their limitations, have historically been and continue to be the primary indicator of student performance and learning in college (Lavin, 1965; Walvoord and Anderson, 1998). Prompt and authentic feedback on student performance is beneficial for developing realistic student self-appraisals and learning outcomes (Bandura, 1986). To continue serving society in an optimal capacity, colleges and universities need to revisit their practices in assessing student performance. Higher education institutions must understand what grading problems exist and implement effective strategies to deal with the problems accordingly.

What Are the Correlates of College Grades?

College grading is an exceptionally complex phenomenon. What factors affect college grades? College grades reflect faculty evaluations of student performance in a given environmental context. Theoretical and empirical analyses from different disciplines indicate that students' performance is related to both who the students are and what the students do in college. The literature suggests that faculty background and environmental contexts, including the broad social, institutional, and disciplinary settings, influence faculty evaluations of student performances. Therefore, student course grades are correlated with factors concerning characteristics of the student, faculty, course, discipline, and institution, among others. A longitudinal understanding of the change in college grades thus has to do with changes in student and faculty populations, student course-taking patterns, and institutional, disciplinary, and broad social contexts.

What Is the College Grading Problem?

This report presents a conceptual framework that can aid in understanding the complexity of grading problems in higher education. It contends that college grades should be analyzed at different levels and asserts that the grading problem includes a set of subproblems. The conceptual framework proposes that grades at different levels—individual course grades, student grade point averages (GPAs), and institutional GPAs—are distinct indicators of different college grading policies and practices. National and campuswide GPAs have been under scrutiny for decades. To understand why institutional GPAs change over time, it is necessary to understand the problems in individual course grading, students' choice of coursework, and changes in student populations, among other factors.

Grade inflation is at the center of the college grading controversy (Rosovsky and Hartley, 2002). Inflation can be explicit or implicit or both. Explicit grade inflation specifically refers to the phenomenon of students with comparable backgrounds and performance receiving higher grades than their counterparts in previous cohorts from faculty members of similar backgrounds. Implicit grade inflation may result from changes in faculty characteristics, institutional policies, and other factors. Grade increase, although constantly misrepresented as an indication of grade inflation, indicates that average grades increase over time. Grade compression refers to the phenomenon of the diminishing discriminating function of grades on student performance. When a severe grade inflation problem exists, grades can be compressed so much that grades no longer differentiate student performance at a desirable level. Grading disparity points to the problem of substantially different grading standards enacted in different courses and in different academic disciplines. Thus, the grading problem in colleges and universities is a problem set comprising all four of these intertwined subproblems.

What Are the Problems Associated with College Grading?

Based on the proposed conceptual framework on college grading, this report develops a better understanding of the changing pattern of college grades over time. Although somewhat divergent and clearly time dependent, the empirical evidence confirms that institutional GPAs are trending upward. Further, this upward trend appears to be more pronounced in available empirical evidence regarding individual campuses than in the nation as a whole.

Although numerous outcries have been raised about grade inflation, the empirical data supporting grade inflation appear to be moderate, with only minimal evidence maintaining that explicit grade inflation is extensive in colleges and universities. Implicit grade inflation, however, receives a stronger empirical confirmation. Grading disparity among different courses appears to be a more serious problem. Coupled with changes in students' choice of courses (partially as a result of differential incentives from grading disparity), grading disparity becomes the mechanism that drives up individual student GPAs and institutional GPAs.

Although it is widely believed that both changes in college grades and grade inflation could lead to the diminishing power of grades in differentiating students (Mansfield, 2001), empirical evidence in the literature does not support the argument that grade compression is at work. It should be no surprise that grade compression might be inevitable if college grades continue to rise.

What Causes Changes in College Grades?

The underlying forces on the upward trend of college grades are complex. Student grades in individual courses are determined by a series of factors related to the student, faculty member, course, and discipline. Student GPA is a mathematical composite of a student's grades in coursework, embedded in the cultural and contextual conditions of the college in a given historical time period (Birnbaum, 1977). College-level GPAs, in turn, depend on what GPAs students earn and what types of students enroll in college. Grading practices such as grading disparity and grade inflation are the primary changeable mechanisms that drive up institutional GPAs. Other factors, such as changes in the social and cultural context and changes in the student population, have substantial influence on college grades but are less subject to manipulation and administration by higher education institutions.

The primary causes of grade inflation are student evaluations of teaching (Johnson, 2003), "the disengagement compact" between the faculty and student (Kuh, 1999, 2003), and state merit-based financial aid programs (Sloop, 2000). All three interpretations are related to faculty grading practices. It is alleged that faculty members may distribute higher grades in exchange for better student evaluations of teaching effectiveness. Additionally, the increasing emphasis on research and the concurrent decreasing importance placed on teaching lead to faculty disengagement. Further exacerbating the grading problem is students' increasing focus on attaining top-notch grades rather than on acquiring knowledge. In an environment where state-sponsored merit aid programs exist, faculty members may become reluctant to give lower grades for fear of jeopardizing students' eligibility for state financial aid. In addition to differences in grading philosophy, disciplinary culture, and enrollment pressures, the difference in costs to faculty members in terms of the demand on time and energy in more accurate grading appears to be the main cause for grading disparity in different courses and in different disciplines.

How Can Colleges and Universities Deal with Grading Problems?

Colleges and universities need to pay attention to two existing problems that can directly influence grading practices in undergraduate education: grading disparity and grade inflation. Effective grading practices need to be vigorous and fair and conducive to student learning (Walvoord and Anderson, 1998). Over decades, innovative practices have emerged on campuses. An achievement index, for example, has been proposed to deal with grading disparity among different disciplines within institutions. Expanded contextual transcripts fight against the grade inflation problem; however, corrective technical procedures should only be used as a last resort. Higher education administrators can adopt appropriate policy instruments suitable for institutional contexts to achieve goals of promoting good practices in college grading.

What Are the Implications for Research and Practice?

Effective policies for addressing college grading problems need to be based on conceptual and empirical evidence and targeted toward specific grading problems (Krathwohl, 1997; Slavin, 2002). Similarly, research on college grading problems needs to be conceptually and empirically solid to support evidence-based policy discussions. This report aids in gaining a better understanding of grading problems in colleges and designing more effective policies and practices in preventing and correcting these problems in higher education.

Foreword

A perennial concern in higher education is educational quality. One traditional marker of quality is the grading system. Students who demonstrate excellent work receive higher grades. This concept seems simple enough, yet notions and standards of grading vary by educational context and among individuals with differing philosophies. Some people do not believe grades are part of the equation of educational quality, while others believe it is the most important indicator. Grading, often assumed to be a well understood practice, is very complex and misunderstood. Nevertheless, campuses hardly ever have substantive discussions about grades. Instead, faculty bemoan the rise in grading, and administrators find themselves paralyzed to act on a process largely in the hands of individual faculty. One of the current complexities that institutions face is a perceived rise in grades—grade inflation—that challenges educational notions of quality. In this monograph, Dr. Shouping Hu examines the complex issue of grading, asking several tough questions: Do grades accurately measure performance? How have student evaluations of teaching affected grading practices? Do faculty and students have an implicit compact that faculty put little effort into teaching and in exchange lower their expectations of students? Do scholarship programs and the award of state aid based on merit alter grading practices? Is grade inflation the real problem, or is it grade disparity? These provocative questions are addressed with solid data and research, making this a significant addition to the literature.

A major contribution of this monograph is the conceptual framework used to analyze college grades, which takes into account individual course-grading philosophy, students' choice of coursework, changes in composition of the faculty, and changes in the student population, among other factors. The conceptual

---

framework helps professionals to understand that grading practices need to be examined at multiple levels, not just in the aggregate at the institutional and national levels. Practices and problems vary by discipline, institutional type, faculty rank, and other such conditions. The framework also provides advice about where policymakers and leaders can target efforts (state aid policy) and other areas where they can have little or no impact (student demographic shifts). Another contribution is the practical advice for professionals. A very interesting approach is capitalizing on the knowledge that senior faculty have related to grading. These individuals are a wealth of knowledge about changing institutional practices, fluctuations in departmental and school norms, and various strategies for grading. Dr. Hu also suggests the need for institutional policies related to grading and more discussion on campuses about standards and norms. The primary message of this monograph is that grading is a shared responsibility among members of the institution and external players such as accreditation bodies, state governments, and boards of trustees. Systematic work across these various groups is necessary to change the context that rewards lenient grading.

Those interested in this subject may want to consider other ASHE Higher Education Reports. Braxton, Luckey, and Helland's *Institutionalizing a Broader View of Scholarship* explores new visions of faculty work that provide an approach for how faculty might become involved in discussions of grading. Jones offers advice on grading practices and norms within professional fields in *Transforming the Curriculum*. Frost's *Academic Advising for Student Success* provides another tool for examining the issue of grading through the way students are advised into majors. And *Retaining Minority Students in Higher Education* by Swail, Redd, and Perna describes the importance of systematic approaches to change in institutional policy so that minority students are not unduly affected.

Discussions of grading will lead to much needed discussions of educational philosophy. Too often, institutions operate on unexamined assumptions that are damaging to students. It is time to collectively explore grading and educational quality and come up with a response that makes sense in the current content.

Adrianna J. Kezar
Series Editor

Acknowledgments

I am indebted to many people who helped me in various ways during the preparation of this report. My interest in grading problems in higher education started from a collaborative project with George Kuh when I was a graduate student. In 1998, George asked me to do an analysis on student self-reported grades using data from the College Student Experience Questionnaire Research Program at Indiana University. We eventually published the study in *Educational Evaluation and Policy Analysis* to explain what contributes to the increase in college grades over time. We then received numerous notes from interested readers offering their opinions and anecdotes regarding grading problems. Because debates on college grading problems continue and confusions remain, I decided to conduct a definitive analysis on this topic in 2003. My mentors at Indiana University, Edward St. John, Don Hossler, and George Kuh, graciously offered useful comments and suggestions on my proposal to the ASHE Higher Education Report series. I am grateful for their support of this project and many of my other endeavors. Marty Finkelstein at Seton Hall University carefully read both the proposal and the draft of the report. His insightful comments helped me refine the arguments in this report. Comments and suggestions from the anonymous reviewers were extremely helpful in improving the quality of the final product. Many colleagues and friends from the Overseas Chinese Association for Institutional Research critiqued the idea for this project and offered good advice for revising the first draft. Series editor

Adrianna Kezar provided much needed encouragement and support throughout the whole process. I gratefully acknowledge the contributions from all these professional colleagues and friends. I especially want to thank my wife Shaoqing and my son Alex for the joy and happiness they bring into my professional and personal life.

Grading Problems in Higher Education

COLLEGE GRADES and grading practices constantly spark controversy both inside and outside the academy. Concerns about the continuing increase of college grades are found in the general press and academic journals, and on the Internet (Birnbaum, 1977; Juola, 1976; Kuh and Hu, 1999; Levine and Cureton, 1998; Rojstaczer, 2003; Rosovsky and Hartley, 2002). These concerns are particularly evident in the sharp criticism aimed at grade inflation during recent years. One observer claimed that today "A is average" (Pedersen, 1997, p. 64). At Princeton, the class of 1997's median GPA was 3.42, in contrast to 3.08 for the class of 1973 (Archibold, 1998). In 2003, A's accounted for 47 percent of Princeton's undergraduate grades, up from 31 percent in 1970 (Arenson, 2004). This outcome is by no means unique to Princeton. Harvard University has also been discussed in the media for its widely disclosed and hotly debated problem of grade inflation. Headlines such as "Harvard's Quiet Secret: Rampant Grade Inflation" (Healy, 2001) divulge the atmosphere surrounding this topic and the embarrassing nature of grade inflation to universities. One harsh comment about this phenomenon came from a Harvard insider. "But at Harvard, the supposed pinnacle of American education, professors are quite satisfied to bestow outlandishly high grades upon students. . . . There is something inappropriate—almost sick—in the spectacle of mature adults showering young people with unbelievable praise" (Mansfield, 2001, p. B24).

Currently, the crusade against grade inflation is occurring in a new arena. Rojstaczer, a professor at Duke University, started using the Internet to take on issues in college grading (2003). He collected institutional average grades

FIGURE 1

Trends in College-Level Average GPAs from 1991–92 to 2001–02

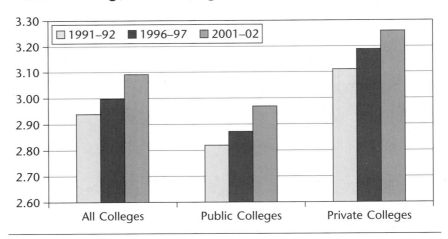

SOURCE: Rojstaczer, 2003.

from a large number of colleges and universities and demonstrated that college grades were on the rise in the 1990s (Figure 1). The upward trend was similar in both public and private institutions, but the average grades were higher in the private institutions (Rojstaczer, 2003). Believing that grade inflation is now a part of academic life, critics of grade inflation question whether the academy is doing "the right thing" (Rosovsky and Hartley, 2002) and urge that "it's time to face the facts" of grade inflation in American higher education (Mansfield, 2001).

Not everyone agrees there is rampant grade inflation in higher education. Some argue that the report on college grade inflation itself is inflated (Adelman, 1995a, 1995b, 1996, 1999a, 1999b, 2001; Shoichet, 2002). A national report released by the U.S. Department of Education on college students in 1999–2000 (Horn, Peter, Rooney, and Malizio, 2002) indicates that a substantial portion of students received grades of C's and D's (Table 1). In total, 33.5 percent of recent undergraduate students received a GPA of C's, D's, or lower at the national level, whereas about 14.5 percent of students received mostly A's, directly contradicting the assertion made by critics of grade inflation that grades of C's and D's were nearly obsolete in college grading practices.

TABLE 1
Percentages of Undergraduates Achieving Grade Point Averages Shown, 1999–2000

	C's and D's or Lower	B's and C's	Mostly B's	A's and B's	Mostly A's
Total	33.50	16.40	24.60	10.90	14.50
By type of institution attended					
Public four-year	34.40	21.20	25.10	9.70	9.70
Private nonprofit four-year	22.40	18.20	30.10	14.40	15.00
Public two-year	38.20	13.20	22.30	9.80	16.60
All private for-profit	25.60	12.10	23.80	16.20	22.30
By class level					
Graduating senior	15.80	21.90	34.50	14.70	13.00
All other undergraduates	35.40	15.80	23.60	10.50	14.70
By sex					
Men	38.80	16.60	22.60	9.60	12.40
Women	29.40	16.20	26.20	12.00	16.20
By racial and ethnic group					
One race					
American Indian	41.80	16.90	23.30	9.70	8.30
Asian	32.20	17.70	26.40	10.10	13.60
Black	48.90	16.00	20.30	7.50	7.30
Native Hawaiian or other Pacific Islander	39.60	19.70	22.30	9.70	8.70
White	30.30	16.20	25.30	11.70	16.50
Other	39.30	17.80	24.30	9.50	9.00
More than one race	34.00	15.80	25.80	11.90	12.50
Hispanic (may be any race)	41.80	16.70	23.70	8.30	9.60
By dependent status					
Financially dependent on parents	38.20	18.80	25.20	9.40	8.40
Financially independent	29.00	14.00	24.10	12.40	20.60
By age as of December 31, 1999					
18 or younger	42.60	14.70	23.40	9.40	10.00
19 to 23	38.10	19.00	25.10	9.40	8.30
24 to 29	33.30	16.90	24.70	10.30	14.90
30 to 39	23.10	13.20	25.90	14.80	23.00
40 and older	20.10	10.10	22.00	14.80	33.00

SOURCE: Chronicle of Higher Education, 2003.

Some argue that grade inflation in higher education is a "dangerous myth" because the discussed phenomenon has been accepted on faith, not on the basis of data and reasoned analysis: "Yet on campuses across America today, academe's usual requirements for supporting data and reasoned analysis have been suspended for some reason where this issue is concerned. It is largely accepted on faith that grade inflation—an upward shift in students' grade-point averages without a similar rise in achievement—exists, and that it is a bad thing. Meanwhile, the truly substantive issues surrounding grades and motivation have been obscured or ignored" (Kohn, 2002, p. B7).

Adelman (2001, 2004b) warns that the general public's impression about higher education has been shaped by anecdotes from a few elite institutions such as Harvard and Princeton. "The case for grade inflation in U.S. higher education that is played out in the media is not based on anything you or I would regard as inflation. Rather, it is a story of the distribution of traditional letter grades without any reference to either the methods or criteria by which the grades were assigned or of the subjects in which they were given. No one asks whether all those 'As' were given in Recreation or Chemistry" (Adelman, 2001, p. 25).

The controversy over grade inflation in college is not likely to disappear in the foreseeable future. It is evident that this topic has attained mythic status and constantly intrigues people, both inside and outside the ivory tower. As accountability becomes one of the major policy issues in higher education (Heller, 2000; Naughton, Suen, and Shavelson, 2003; Shavelson and Huang, 2003), it is time to demystify the grade inflation phenomenon and unravel various grading problems in higher education.

Assessment of College Student Learning

In the foreword to the conference program of the 2003 annual meeting of the American Educational Research Association, Herman and Linn (2003) state, "Accountability has become a catchword for the new century, a dominant theme in the continuing public dialogue about education and its improvement. Calls for rigorous standards and evidence of their accomplishment have been echoed in legislative mandates across the country" (p. 3). The public historically has cherished American colleges and universities, considering them some of the greatest social institutions in American society (Altbach, Berdahl, and Gumport, 1998; Altbach, Gumport, and Johnstone, 2001). Individual students, their families, and the society invest tremendous resources in higher education (Paulsen and Smart, 2002). In turn, they expect colleges and universities to maximize student learning and personal development and to advance societal well-being (Altbach, Berdahl, and Gumport, 1998; Hu and Kuh, 2003).

Unfortunately, relatively little is known about how well colleges fulfill their principal goal of educating students. For instance, the *Measuring Up* reports issued by the National Center for Public Policy and Higher Education (2001, 2002) awarded an "incomplete" for student learning on state-by-state report cards. This rating continues to be true, even though efforts are under way in a number of states to assess college student learning (National Center for Public Policy and Higher Education, 2004). Without other reliable information about student learning, college grades remain the primary indicator of students' academic performance. Not only do employers and graduate school admissions officers continue to consider college grades an indicator of student performance; educational researchers also have constantly used student GPAs as a measure of academic performance or achievement (Milton, Pollio, and Eison, 1986). Even though grades might be "inadequate, imprecise, and wildly idiosyncratic indicators of learning" (Angelo in Walvoord and Anderson, 1998, p. xi), various groups, including students, parents, and business recruiters, place considerable faith in grades as a way to communicate student characteristics and performance (Milton, Pollio, and Eison, 1986). To appropriately assess and substantially improve student learning in college, it is necessary to accurately identify problems in college grading practices and design effective policies to correct and prevent grading problems and optimize student learning.

Purpose

College grades play important educational and social roles (Milton, Pollio, and Eison, 1986; Walvoord and Anderson, 1998). What is not well understood are the types of problems that exist in college grading practices. Conversations about grade inflation in higher education are often based on sparse anecdotal evidence and charged with value judgments and opinions (Adelman, 2001; Hu, 2003). Participants may speak to the problem of grade inflation and use the same words; however, they may inadvertently be using the same language to describe different phenomena. Therefore, the first purpose of this report is to delineate a conceptual framework to help understand various grading problems in college. Without a shared frame of reference, conversations about grade inflation are likely to be unproductive and possibly counterproductive. Second, this report summarizes empirical evidence about college grades and grading practices through the use of the proposed conceptual framework. Third, this report aims to reconcile the conflicting arguments about college grades. The underlying forces responsible for the grading problem are also identified. Last, the emerging practices and innovative proposals used to address the varied problems surrounding grade inflation are discussed.

Overview and Scope

This report intends to refine the knowledge base related to grading problems so that a shared understanding can be developed. As Krathwohl (1997) suggests, "The development of knowledge results from the creation of a consensus around the interpretation of data in successively widening circles of decreasingly specialized persons" (p. 46). He asserts that both conceptual and empirical evidence are important in making a credible knowledge claim (Krathwohl, 1997). Therefore, this report discusses both conceptual and empirical issues related to college grades and grading practice. Specifically, this report is organized around the following questions:

1. What are the correlates of college grades?
2. What is the grading problem and why should we be concerned about it?
3. What grading problems exist in higher education?
4. What are the causes for different grading problems?
5. What are the strategies that can be used to correct or prevent college grading problems?

It is important to clearly conceptualize and articulate the problem of grade inflation so that the right solutions can be explored. In the current stage of the conversation, much of the debate results from discrepancies in the problem's frame of reference (Adelman, 2004b; Hu, 2003). This report first provides a clear identification of factors that are related to college grades, which is a fundamental step toward a better understanding of grade inflation and contributes to the constructive discussion of grading problems. The report also addresses the confusions of grading problems in higher education and further proposes a conceptual framework that can be used to build a shared understanding of the college grading problem. It furthermore answers the "so what?" question by addressing the consequences of various grading problems. The subsequent section assesses what grading problems exist based on a thorough review of empirical studies. After examining underlying causes for different grading problems, this report explores effective policies and practices to address grading problems in higher education.

Correlates of College Grades

THE CURRENT CONVERSATION focuses on the comparative nature of college grading practices as displayed over time. Participants in the conversation approach issues concerning college grading from a longitudinal standpoint through the comparison of present grades with past grades. For example, critics of grade inflation are worried that the grading practices used in higher education are not as desirable as they used to be. To accurately determine what accounts for the changes, if any, from the past to the present, it is necessary to identify the factors that can influence college grades. It is necessary to review the correlates of college grades from a cross-sectional perspective, which can shed light on the phenomenon of changes in grade over time, because the change of the correlates of college grades may inevitably affect student grades. Cross-sectional analysis provides baseline information for discussions on issues related to college grading problems from a longitudinal perspective.

College grading is an exceptionally complex phenomenon because it is subject to both external social forces and internal changes of the participants (for example, students and faculty), policies and practices (for example, grading policies), and other factors (Birnbaum, 1977). Thus, a variety of factors can affect student grades in college. Without a clear understanding of factors related to individual grades and a thorough discussion about the changing nature of those factors over time, one is unlikely to decipher the facts from the myths in the college grading controversy (Chen and Cheng, 1999).

To understand college grading, researchers and scholars adopted different disciplinary perspectives to study and interpret college grades (Kuh and Hu, 1999;

Walvoord and Anderson, 1998). Economists view grades as a reward for academic performance, which is assumed to be related to individual academic ability as well as the quantity and quality of effort the student puts forth in educational activities (Becker, 1965; Hanushek, 1979). As a type of reward for academic performance, college grades serve as incentives for students in allocating their time and effort. Measures of students' ability and investment of their time and effort in the educational process are considered in econometric analysis of college grades. Sociologists typically assume that background characteristics have a nontrivial direct effect on academic achievement. Therefore, it is accepted that student backgrounds such as gender, race, and ethnicity and socioeconomic status need to be considered in understanding academic performance and college grades (Coleman, Hoffer, and Kilgore, 1982; Farkas and Hotchkiss, 1989; Van-Laar, Sidanius, Rabinowitz, and Sinclair, 1999). Psychologists suggest that motivation, self-efficacy, and other psychological variables all make differences in individual achievement and grades (Bandura, 1994; Marsh and Roche, 2000; McKeachie and others, 1990). Educational researchers frequently use a combination of disciplinary perspectives when examining problems such as grade inflation in higher education (Kuh and Hu, 1999; Shavelson and Huang, 2003; Wood, Ridley, and Summerville, 1999).

To identify the correlates of college grades, both the participants in the grading process and the environmental contexts contribute to the final product—college grades. Student grades in a given course are an indicator of student performance in the eyes of the faculty member. For this reason, students, faculty, contextual measures of the course, discipline, and the institution are major components in determining college grades and explaining the differences among college grades (Figure 2). Social contexts outside higher education can influence college grading, but outside social influences are largely beyond the control of a higher education institution. Inside the higher education system, the institution and academic discipline are two primary organizational formats that affect academic activities and grading practices (Clark, 1983). In a time of increasing concern about grade inflation, doubts arise concerning the validity of using grades as an indicator of student performance. Yet there remains no other direct measure of student performance. Further investigation into grading issues might benefit from the review of five

FIGURE 2
The Determinants of Student Course Grade

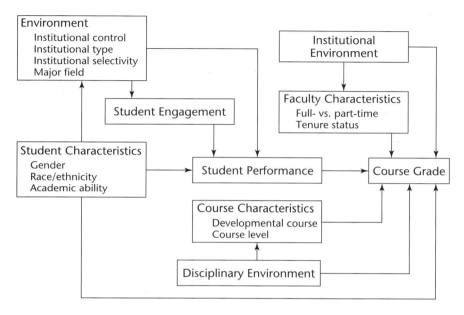

clusters of factors relating to student course grades: the student, the faculty, the course, the discipline, and the institution.

Students

Student characteristics have a substantial impact on college grades. Student ability, gender, and socioeconomic status (SES) are the basic correlates of college grades, as these three factors are consistently related to students' academic performance (Lavin, 1965). Specifically, student "ability is directly related to school performance; females have higher levels of academic achievement than males; and students of higher SES perform at higher levels than students of lower SES" (p. 43). Differences are likewise seen in gender. Studies have consistently shown that female students receive higher grades than their male counterparts (Adelman, 1999a; Goldman, 1985; Kuh and Hu, 1999; Volkwein and others, 2000). Student race/ethnicity is also related to college grades. Minority students are found to receive lower grades after controlling for other related factors (Farkas and Hotchkiss, 1989; Van-Laar, Sidanius, Rabinowitz, and Sinclair, 1999).

Traditional predictors such as SAT/ACT scores, students' socioeconomic status, and high school grades are moderately associated with college grades (Robbins and others, 2004); however, SAT/ACT scores and high school grades are consistently the strongest predictors of student GPA in college, among all factors. Further, some psychosocial factors affect students' college grades. Academic self-efficacy appears to be the best predictor of GPA, with the second best predictor being achievement motivation. Other factors such as financial support, academic goals, academic-related skills, and social involvement are also found to have some impact on GPA. Student year in college (class level) likewise affects student grades. In general, lower-division students tend to receive weaker grades.

Regarding the relationship between student grades and student college behavior (that is, students' effort and engagement in college activities), research results provide somewhat conflicting information. Recent literature suggests a relationship exists between student effort and college grades, even though the magnitude of this relationship is debatable (Kuh and Hu, 1999; Rau and Durand, 2000; Schuman, 2001). Frisbee (1984) examined a random sample of 222 students at Cornell University and found that the time students allocated to a course was significantly and positively associated with the grade earned. Schuman, Walsh, Olson, and Etheridge (1985) reported that a positive correlation existed between hours of study and grades but that it was generally very small and largely limited to students who spent above-average amounts of time studying. Volkwein and others (2000) reported that student effort is a strong predictor of student GPA. They also found that favorable classroom experiences contributed to higher GPA.

Faculty

Faculty members have the primary responsibility in assessing student academic performance and assigning grades to students. Faculty backgrounds appear to matter somewhat in assigning grades to students. Adjunct faculty members tend to distribute higher grades than regular faculty (Chen and Cheng, 1999;

Sonner, 2000). Adjunct professors, hired on a term-by-term basis, are more likely to be pressured to attain positive student evaluations and thus distribute higher grades. The credentials of the instructor do not appear to make substantial differences in student grades, however. Faculty rank has marginal impact on grading practice (Chen and Cheng, 1999), but faculty tenure status influences grading practices. Untenured faculty members are more likely to assign higher grades to students than tenured faculty members who teach similar courses (Moore and Trahan, 1998).

Courses

Courses impact college grades in several ways. Different levels of courses create differences in student grades. The higher the course level, the higher the grades (Chen and Cheng, 1999; Sonner, 2000); the smaller the class, the higher the grades (Sonner, 2000). Developmental courses may be awarded higher grades. Additionally, students' independent work in the junior or senior years tends to receive higher grades than regular courses.

Discipline

Academic disciplines and major fields can have substantial differences in grading practices. Grades for courses in the humanities and social sciences generally are higher than grades in other fields (Johnson, 2003; Kuh and Hu, 1999). Fields related to science and mathematics tend to have rigorous grading practices (Willingham, Lewis, Morgan, and Ramist, 1990). Willingham, Lewis, Morgan, and Ramist's study revealed that biology, physical science, engineering, and calculus had the strictest grading policies, whereas physical education, studio art, music, theater, and education maintained lenient grading systems.

Institution

Institutional characteristics influence grading practices. Grades are not uniformly awarded across institutional types. Public institutions tend to award lower grades compared with their private counterparts. Students at different Carnegie-type institutions receive different grades. Students at doctoral universities tend to receive the highest grades compared with students enrolled in other types of schools (Kuh and Hu, 1999). In addition, selective colleges maintain lower college GPAs when controlling for other factors (Volkwein and others, 2000).

Numerous factors can interact, making college grading a complex phenomenon. For example, male students at research universities report grades equal to those of females, while male students at all other types of institutions have significantly lower grades than their female counterparts. White students uniformly earn higher grades than students of color at all types of institutions. The increase in grades was greater for students in humanities than for science and mathematics majors from the mid-1980s to the mid-1990s. Female students earned higher grades in all the major field clusters, with the gender difference most pronounced in the preprofessional and humanities fields (Kuh and Hu, 1999).

The apparent lack of other direct measures on students' performance elicits an interesting problem. "There is no reliable way to determine the changing quality of undergraduate work that lies behind the grade. One would need, subject by subject, samples of student work responding to the same 'prompts,' judged by the same faculty members using the same criteria, over two or three decades in order to determine the changing relationship between grades and performance" (Adelman, 1999a, p. 198).

In reality, researchers usually use proxy measures of student performance in examining grading problems. GRE or other standardized test scores have been used as the underlying measures to explore the grade inflation problem (Wood, Ridley, and Summerville, 1999). Student academic ability and engagement in college are important determinants in academic performance (Pascarella and Terenzini, 1991). Researchers also use student academic ability as measured by the ACT or SAT along with student engagement measures to examine college grading problems (Kuh and Hu, 1999; McSpirit and Jones, 1999).

In sum, cross-sectional analyses reveal that college grades are influenced by a variety of factors: the characteristics of the student, faculty, course, institution, and the discipline. Undoubtedly, changes in the determinants of college grades could impact grades over time. This understanding forms a foundation for an improved conceptualization of grading problems in higher education.

Reframing the College Grading Problem

GRADE INFLATION is a common term used to describe a problem in college grading. Inflation itself is a term borrowed from the discipline of economics with special reference to price inflation. Price inflation refers to the increases in price over time when the purchasing power of money is falling. Price inflation represents a process in which a given amount of goods and services has increased in cost over a specified period of time relative to a base period (Wegman, 1987). Then, by definition, grade inflation refers to the increase of grades over a specified period of time with higher grades being awarded for the same quality of work.

Accordingly, two types of analytical strategies are used to demonstrate the problem of grade inflation. The first one presents information concerning the increase of average grades over time (see, for example, Astin, 1997; Rojstaczer, 2003). This strategy argues that if average grades go up over time, one can assume that grade inflation exists. The second approach is to present a change in grade distribution over time (Astin, 1997; Levine and Cureton, 1998). If the percentage of students who receive A's and B's increases while the percentage of students receiving C's and D's decreases, grade inflation may be present.

Others argue that the simple upward trend of college grades cannot be considered evidence of grade inflation (Birnbaum, 1977; Kuh and Hu, 1999). They argue that concerns about grade inflation are warranted only if evidence suggests that higher grades are undeserved. Two aspects have been advanced from this line of reasoning. First, inflation needs to be discussed in relation to some underlying measure of the quality of student work or student performance. In the event that the measuring of the quality of student work is not available, it is desirable to consider factors that might contribute to the quality of student work, such as student academic ability or effort. Without an original meritorious measure, the discussion of grade inflation is unproductive or even counterproductive (Adelman, 1999b; Kuh and Hu, 1999). Second, because many factors can contribute to college grades, it is necessary to use a multivariate approach to understand the change in college grades (Birnbaum, 1977; Kuh and Hu, 1999). Commonly examined factors are student background characteristics (gender, race/ethnicity, socioeconomic status), academic preparation (SAT scores), academic performance out of college (GRE scores), effort on educationally purposeful activities, and inflation in college grading practice (Birnbaum, 1977). Therefore, grade inflation may be at work for the current generation if the grading standard has changed over time. Other factors need to be controlled for examining the change in grades over time (Birnbaum, 1977; Kuh and Hu, 1999).

The grade inflation phenomenon can be conceptualized in two different ways (Hu and Kuh, 1998; Koretz and Berends, 2001; Kuh and Hu, 1999). One is the commonly termed "mean-shift" grade inflation phenomenon—a change in average grades for students with a given level of preparation, effort, or performance in different time periods (Figure 3). This notion of "grade inflation" suggests only a shift upward in college grades over time, but the relationship between grades and the underlying measures (for example, academic performance) remains essentially intact. The other conceptualization recognizes that the relationship between grades and the underlying measure for grading (for example, student effort or academic performance) may change significantly over time. Specifically, Koretz and Berends (2001) suggest that a weaker relationship between grades and the underlying measure, such as academic performance or a decreased correlation, could be considered as an indication of grade inflation (Figure 4). This outcome is consistent with Kuh and Hu's notion (1999) of return of grades for student effort. Kuh and Hu (1999) suggest that if increasing efforts put forth by students have not resulted in a discernible increase in grades students receive, grade inflation might be at work. This type of grade inflation functions as making grades less differentiating on the important meritorious measures—a phenomenon also commonly

FIGURE 3
"Mean Shift" in Grades: Grade Inflation

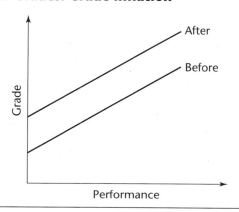

SOURCE: Koretz and Berends, 2001.

FIGURE 4
"Decreased Correlation" Between Grades and Performance: Grade Compression

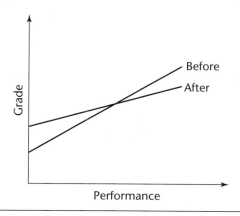

SOURCE: Koretz and Berends, 2001.

known as *grade compression* (Hu and Kuh, 1998; Kuh and Hu, 1999). In general, the mean-shift type of grade inflation suggests that there is room for average grades to rise, probably as a result of the relatively low average of grades awarded to prior cohorts. The "decreased correlation" type of grade inflation in most cases may suggest that there is not much room in the grading scheme for average grades to keep increasing. Because there is a finite upper limit in grades, the mean-shift type of grade inflation will inevitably become a grade compression mechanism and end with the decreased correlation type of grade inflation.

Therefore, grade inflation is just one aspect of the college-grading problem. Strictly speaking, an increase in college grades itself is not necessarily a problem, as long as this increase is accompanied with a proper increase in student performance or other types of meritorious indicators. In reality, grade increases might be a symptom of an underlying grade inflation problem, even though these two phenomena may not necessarily be related. Grade inflation could undermine the educational and social functions of grades and therefore warrant serious attention. The first type of grade inflation where a uniform upward drift exists is the mean-shift type of grade inflation. In this report, grade inflation specifically refers to this type of inflation. The second type of grade inflation, given that grades have an upper limit, is the decreased correlation type of grade inflation. It is referred to as *grade compression* in this report (Hu and Kuh, 1998; Kuh and Hu, 1999; Rosovsky and Hartley, 2002). The grade compression process alters relative awards to different work and performance. At the extreme of grade compression (where all students get A's), college grades "yield no information whatsoever" *(The Economist,* 2002, p. 74). In addition, changes in course requirements and in students' choice of courses coupled with grading disparities in different disciplines complicate the conversation on college grading problems. It is critical to use different terms carefully in order to clarify the subtle differences and establish constructive communications (Table 2).

In addition to the distinction in the various types of college grading problems, it is important to articulate the meaning of "grade" to unravel the complexity of the problem and to explore appropriate solutions. It is necessary to differentiate concepts of grade inflation and GPA inflation, because these two phenomena are different processes with distinct causes (Birnbaum, 1977). Grade inflation is a process implying that a given level of academic achievement is awarded a higher grade for current cohorts than previous

TABLE 2
Comparison of Different Types of Grading Problems

Grading Problem	Indication	Consequence
Grade Increase	Average grades in a given course increase over time.	Grade increase itself is not necessarily a problem, as long as this increase is accompanied with proper increases in student performance or other types of meritorious indicators. However, it could be a symptom of other types of grading problems such as grade inflation.
Grade Inflation	Similar quality of academic performance in a given course is awarded higher grades at the present time than before. It refers to a "mean shift" upward in student grades in the given coursework.	Grade inflation favors recent generations over previous ones because it violates horizontal equity criteria. It also undermines the motivational function of grades in student learning processes and academic achievement.
Grade Compression	Variations in student course grades are limited so much that grades can no longer differentiate student performance. It refers to a "decreased correlation" in student course grades and underlying meritorious measures such as student academic performance.	Grade compression diminishes the function of grades in differentiating students' academic performance and effort and violates vertical equity in college grading processes. Academic performance is rewarded relatively less because the rate of return of performance in grades diminishes in the compression process.
Grading Disparity	Similar academic performances may be rewarded differently in different courses or in different academic units.	Grading disparity affects student course choices in college and can also lead to GPA and grade inflation.

cohorts. GPA inflation, on the other hand, refers to the increase in the mean rating of a number of courses statistically aggregated. It may be related to grade inflation in individual courses, and it may also be related to courses included in the statistical calculation. Further, it is subject to a range of institutional policies and practices that govern the approaches to the inclusion of courses and the statistical methods of calculating GPA. In fact, the phenomenon of GPA inflation may not be the inflation of grades on individual courses but rather issues of disparity in grading practices among different disciplines and student course choice (Johnson, 2003; Mitchell, 1998; Prather, Smith, and Kodras, 1979). Even when no grade inflation exists for individual courses, GPA inflation is possible if students select courses that tend to award higher grades as a result of grading disparities in courses (Prather, Smith, and Kodras, 1979). For this reason, Prather, Smith, and Kodras (1979) suggest that "GPA is a low reliable measure to use in determining how grades are changing" (p. 20). Other scholars endorse this viewpoint through their independent work. Cunningham and Lawson (1979) assert that university-wide GPAs could be misleading in part when different departments within the same university use different grading standards and when grades from other courses are heterogeneous (Goldman and Slaughter, 1976; Goldman and Widawski, 1976).

Guiding Conceptual Framework

In this report, the concepts of grade increase, grade inflation, grade compression, and grading disparity are used as distinct terms, although they are intricately related. The following conceptual framework incorporates previous discussions on the complexity of college grading problems (Figure 5). Several fundamental propositions emerge from the guiding conceptual framework.

First, college grades should be analyzed on different levels, with grading problems being considered as multiple-layer phenomena. Current studies acknowledge that a major concern exists with the rising trend of institution-level average GPAs. Given that institution-level average GPAs are essentially functions of individual student GPAs and various student characteristics, the

FIGURE 5
Guiding Conceptual Framework: The Interrelations of Grading Problems

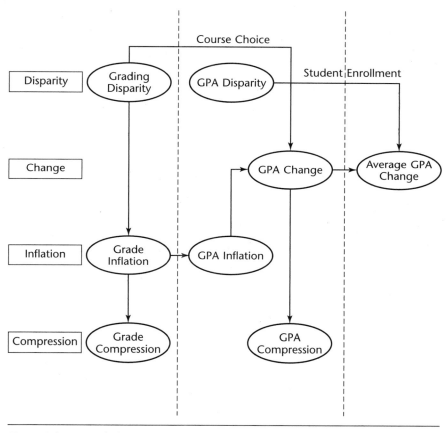

Note: → indicates causal relations.

discussions concerning the increase in institution-level average GPAs can be linked to changes in individual student GPAs over time. This phenomenon is better examined on the student level. If average individual GPAs increase, GPA compression may result—a diminishing power of grades in differentiating students. Individual student GPAs depend on both the grading practices in individual courses and the portfolio of courses the student has taken. Thus, investigating grading practices within courses (grade inflation) and between courses (grading disparity) is necessary to unravel the complexity of the grading problem. A course-level analysis on grading practices is necessary to reveal grading problems at both the individual course level and the institutional level.

Second, given the limitation of GPA as an indicator of grading practice, course-level grades are more accurately indicative of grading practices in higher education. Even though considerable attention is paid to the changes of institution-level average GPAs, it is the grading patterns at the course level that are of utmost importance. Grade inflation can result from the explicit practice of faculty bestowing higher grades for comparable work previously given lower grades. It can also result from changes in faculty characteristics or changes in institutional policies regarding grading. Grade inflation may lead to the problem of grade compression in a given course inasmuch as grades are based less on student performance. Further, grading disparity could lead to grade inflation because faculty members in courses that traditionally award lower grades may consider themselves to be at a disadvantage.

Third, it is important to take into consideration the changes in student characteristics and student course choice patterns to understand the reasons behind the changes in institution-level average GPAs. Student characteristics are important in determining individual grades, for simply the changes in student population in higher education alter institution-level average grades. If a disparity exists in grading practices between courses, student course choice will vary students' GPAs, which in turn affects institution-level average GPAs.

This guiding conceptual framework differentiates aspects of problems in college grading and delineates their interrelations. Specifically, it acknowledges that grades in different levels reflect diverse aspects of the college grading phenomenon. It further considers grades and GPAs to have different implications for understanding the grading problems, and it articulates the interconnections between grade inflation, grade change (increase), grade compression, and grading disparity.

Consequences of College Grading Problems

It is no surprise that the role of grades in education has been intensely debated; like many other debates, values and ideologies are important (Fowler, 2000). Some scholars view low grades as discouraging students and frustrating their academic progress (Kohn, 1992). Others suggest that it is a distorting, harsh, and punitive practice. Still others are concerned that grades obstruct the improvement of education and hinder at-risk students (Hargis, 1990), thus having undesirable consequences: "grading . . . forecloses on the hopes and aspirations for many students and cosigns them to lower academic ranks, less social status, and reduced employment possibilities before their potential has had a chance to manifest itself" (Edwards, 2000, p. 543).

On the other hand, numerous researchers find that grades have a proper role in the educational process. According to Walvoord and Anderson (1998), "Despite all its problems, grading is still a deeply entrenched mode of evaluating student learning in higher education. It is the basis of a college or university's decision about who graduates. It is the most universal form of communication to employers or graduate schools about the quality of a student's learning" (p. xv). Further, grading has multiple roles in education:

> *In short, we view grading as a context-dependent, complex process that serves multiple roles:*
>
> Evaluation: *the grade purports to be valid, fair, and trustworthy judgment about the quality of the student's work.*
> Communication: *the grade is a communication to the student, as well as to employers, graduate schools, and others. Grading is also the occasion of (sometimes highly emotional) communication and is thus an important and powerful aspect of the ongoing conversation among students and teachers.*
> Motivation: *grading affect how students study, what they focus on, how much time they spend, and how involved they become in the course. Thus grading is a powerful part of the motivational structure of the course, for better or worse.*
> Organization: *a grade on a test or assignment helps to mark transitions, bring closure, and focus effort for both students and teachers. [Walvoord and Anderson, 1998, p. 2]*

Therefore, grades and grading practices serve important educational and social purposes if used properly. Grading process can function as a formative evaluation process so that teaching and learning can be continuously improved (Kuh and Hu, 1999). For instance, faculty can use grades to articulate expectations for performance by clarifying what is expected by way of academic effort to attain certain grades. Faculty can also use grading processes to provide students with feedback as to whether the amount and quality of academic effort they are expending on course-related tasks is sufficient.

Grades can also function as a summative judgment of a student's performance (Kuh and Hu, 1999). The end users of college grades rely on colleges and universities to provide trustworthy information. Employers often use grades in their hiring policies, and graduate schools may use grades for admissions decisions. The soundness of these decisions largely depends on the credibility of the grades' reflecting and differentiating students' performance.

Yet various problems in college grading undermine the proper role of grades in fulfilling these educational and social purposes. "Grade inflation subverts the primary function of grades. Grades are messages. They are means of telling students—and subsequently, parents, employers, and graduate schools—how well or poorly those students have done. A grade that misrepresents a student's performance sends a false message. It tells a lie. The point of using more than one passing grade (usually D through A) is to differentiate levels of successful performance among one's students. Inflating grades to please or encourage students is confusing and ultimately self-defeating" (Kamber and Biggs, 2002, p. B14).

Grade inflation is one of the most troubling phenomena in college grading practice. Grade inflation has ethical implications, for it undermines the values of fairness and equity (Hu, 2003; Wegman, 1987). Two types of equity issues affect policy discussions: horizontal equity and vertical equity. To maintain horizontal equity in grading policies, students with similar performances are awarded similar grades. To uphold vertical equity, students with different performances receive different grades. The higher the student performance, the higher the grade. Grade inflation favors recent generations and thus violates horizontal equity criteria. When grade inflation leads to grade compression, vertical equity is debased, because students of different performance levels receive similar grades.

Grade inflation further undermines the motivational function of grades in the student learning process (Singleton, 1978). Grades can serve as incentives in prioritizing effort placed on academic work, leisure, and other activities (Becker, 1982). Empirical studies suggest that student achievement increases as standards for grading rise, suggesting that students respond favorably to higher academic standards (Betts and Grogger, 2003; Figlio and Lucas, 2000). Studies also suggest that higher standards are more pronounced for students near the top of the achievement distribution than those near the bottom (Betts and Grogger, 2003). If they find that they do not have to exert much effort to receive satisfactory grades, students tend to invest less time and effort in their academic work (Becker, 1982; Betts and Grogger, 2003; Costrell, 1994). Under extreme inflationary conditions, where the majority of students receive A's, the grading system becomes pass-fail (A or F). The pass-fail grading system has multiple drawbacks. Students are less motivated to learn (Karlins, Kaplan, and Stuart, 1969), feel that they learn less (Karlins, Kaplan, and Stuart, 1969), and show lower achievement in pass-fail courses than in regular courses (Gold, Reilly, Silberman, and Lehr, 1971; Karlins, Kaplan, and Stuart, 1969; Von Wittich, 1972). Finally, relative deprivation effects also suggest that grade inflation may, at least temporarily, increase student apprehension to achieve high grades while at the same time devaluing grades as the pressure and need for "good" grades continue (Singleton, 1978).

Grade compression is problematic because it undermines the function of grades in differentiating students' academic performance and effort. It diminishes vertical equity in the college grading process because it decreases the differentiating function of grades. There is no doubt that grades serve multiple purposes, one of which is to differentiate students on the basis of some important meritorious measures such as academic performance. This differentiating function has ethical, academic, and practical implications. It can help enforce a work ethic and build a meritorious academic environment. It can help motivate students to achieve higher levels of academic excellence and maximize student learning out of collegiate experiences. It can also help end users of college grades by accurately informing them about a student's academic achievement in college. Therefore, it is necessary for institutional agents to clarify the expectations for student effort and academic performance for both students and their families through the grading policy and practice. Grade compression, however, undermines these essential functions of grades by discouraging high-ability students to put forth greater efforts in academic activities and thus acts to undermine student learning productivity (Becker, 1982).

The negative consequences of grading disparity are twofold. First, it affects students' course choices in college. As Sabot and Wakeman-Linn (1991) suggest, "Students make their course choices in response to a powerful set of incentives: grades" (p. 160). This separation of high- and low-grading departments and academic disciplines acts as incentives for student course choices (Sabot and Wakeman-Linn, 1991). And it is a main cause for the decline of student enrollment in science and engineering programs. Similarly, Dowd (2000) argues that "relatively low grading quantitative fields and high grading verbal fields create a disincentive for college women to invest in quantitative study." Second, the grading disparity leads to GPA inflation and grade inflation. If students choose to take more courses in high-grading disciplines, their GPAs rise, a phenomenon identified as GPA inflation. Additionally, the disparity between disciplines in grading compels faculty members in low-grading departments to lighten their grading standards (grade inflation) to compete for student enrollment. Grade inflation is contagious and can spread across courses and disciplines.

College grading problems have confounding implications for higher education and for society as a whole. If grading practices do not evaluate students appropriately, colleges and universities are at risk of losing the public trust (Wingspread Group, 1993). Grading problems also undermine the goal of higher education to promote student learning and create human capital (Bowen, 1977). As calls for accountability for student learning intensify (see, for example, Naughton, Suen, and Shavelson, 2003; Shavelson and Huang, 2003), it is time for the academy to reexamine the credibility of college grades in assessing student learning outcomes.

To summarize the complexity surrounding the college grading problem, several things must be considered and articulated so that constructive communications can be initiated and effective solutions explored. First, it is necessary to understand the difference between individual course grade inflation and GPA inflation. One needs to consider grade inflation *within* courses and grading disparity *among* courses. Second, grade increase might be a symptom of grade inflation and warrant legitimate concern; however, grade increase itself is not grade inflation. Further, grade inflation might reduce the differentiating function of grades and lead to grade compression. Researchers and higher education administrators need to understand the complexity and interconnections of the numerous problems of grading to work toward proper corrective measures.

Reexamining the Empirical Evidence

THE LACK OF a common frame of reference has led to a contentious debate about college grading problems. It is often the case that scholars discuss grade inflation even though they are working with a grade increase issue. The different types of grading problems have diverse causes and consequences and require distinct prevention strategies and remedies.

Grading problems are differentiated into four major types: grade increase, grade inflation, grade compression, and grading disparity. Both grade increase and decrease might raise legitimate concerns about college grading practices. Half a century ago, it was common to hear complaints about the "too stringent" grading practices in higher education (Miller, 1965; Webb, 1959). Yet today the increase in college grades has become a concern. Grade increase is the gross measure of the trend of college grades over time, without consideration of changes in other related factors. Descriptive statistics can show whether an increase in college grades exists. Grade inflation, on the other hand, indicates a "net" increase in grades resulting from changes in grading practices and standards over time, independent of other contributing factors. Therefore, it usually requires multivariate analysis to obtain an accurate answer. Grade inflation usually indicates a tendency toward the lowering of standards in grading practices. Grade compression is the pattern of decreased correlation of college grades and some meritorious measures such as student academic achievement. It is concerned about whether high performance is appropriately awarded and whether grades serve as a useful measure of students' performance. Grading disparity can be seen through the examination of the patterns of grades in different courses and academic disciplines;

however, more sophisticated analysis of grading disparity needs to compare grades in different courses by students of comparable academic ability and preparation.

Grade Increase

Higher education administrators and researchers have been interested in changes in college grades for a long time. When documenting trends of college grades, scholars and researchers choose to focus on higher education as an enterprise to spotlight the national trend, while others working for a given institution are more interested in the institutional pattern of grade change. Data from the institutional study on grades, mostly based on student records, tend to be reliable. Many national studies on college grades use surveys to collect grade information (Hu and Kuh, 1998; Kuh and Hu, 1999; Levine and Cureton, 1998). One exception is a series of studies conducted by Adelman (1999a, 2004b) in which student grades were collected from transcripts as a part of larger projects through the National Center for Education Statistics (NCES).

Available data regarding changes in grades uniformly point to an upward trend in student grades. GPA data for sixteen colleges and universities collected by Rojstaczer (2003) indicate that GPAs increased by 0.5 from 1968 to 2001, with private schools experiencing grade increases at a rate about 25 to 30 percent higher than public schools. The overall tendency for both public and private schools is similarly upward, while private schools have a higher average GPA than public schools. Moreover, the grade gap between private and public institutions is widening. The increase of college grades was "rapid in the 1960s, lulled from the mid-1970s to the mid-1980s, and then took off again" (Rojstaczer, 2003). This observation is consistent with findings in other reports about the changing pattern of college grades (Juola, 1980; Rosovsky and Hartley, 2002).

Although "grade inflation" has been repeatedly used in several national reports on college grades (Juola, 1976, 1980), it is apparent that the phenomenon under discussion is grade increase rather than grade inflation. Juola (1976) found, from surveys of colleges and universities, that the average GPA increased .404 point from 1965 to 1973. A later study showed a .432 rise in GPA from 1960 to 1974, although the increase ceased from 1974 to 1979 (Juola, 1980). Suslow (1977) found similar results in his survey of fifty colleges and universities from 1960 to 1974. Levine and Cureton (1998) found an increasing proportion of students receiving A or higher grades and a decreasing proportion of students receiving C or below from surveys on college students in 1967, 1976, and 1993.

Results from national surveys further indicate that recent cohorts of students report higher college grades than previous generations. Data from student-reported grades in the College Student Experience Questionnaire (CSEQ) demonstrate that "despite lower levels of effort, students are getting higher grades as the fraction of college students reporting B+ or better grades is now at an all-time high" (Kuh, 1999, p. 112). In the 1990s, college students at all institutions reported higher grades. The largest increases in students' reporting B+ or better grades occurred at comprehensive colleges and universities, from 31 percent in the 1980s to 40 percent in the 1990s (Kuh, 1999). This pattern of grade increases is also reflected in the average grades reported by students in all types of institutions and all major fields from the mid-1980s and the mid-1990s (Hu and Kuh, 1998; Kuh and Hu, 1999).

Not everyone agrees, however, that college grades actually increased. In transcript-based studies for the U.S. Department of Education using national data sets, Adelman (1995a, 1999b) found that there were virtually no changes in the distribution of letter grades from 1972 through 1993. Among all institutions in the national surveys, the distribution of grades for two different cohorts, respectively, are as follows: A's—27.3 percent and 25.2 percent, B's—31.2 percent and 31.9 percent, C's—21.9 percent and 22.2 percent, and D's—5.4 percent and 6.0 percent. The remainder of grades are pass-fail and withdrawals. Overall average GPAs in fact declined from 2.71 to 2.65, with an effect size of −.09. Patterns by gender, race/ethnicity, and fields of study varied only slightly. But the distribution of grades in all types of institutions (control, selectivity, and institutional type) showed that a substantial proportion of grades were below B's in those two years. The results of Adelman's study (1995a, 1999b) were corroborated by another recent national study from the

U.S. Department of Education (Horn, Peter, Rooney, and Malizio, 2002). The study reported that although 14.5 percent of students received mostly A's, more than a third had received grades of C or below in 1999 to 2000. Thus, the fluctuation of college grades over different time periods is apparent.

> *Judging by both distribution of letter grades and GPAs, changes have been minor and complex since the high school class of 1972 went to college. In terms of the distribution of letter grades, the proportion of grades that were "A" declined slightly between the Class of 1972 and the Class of 1982, then rose between the Class of 1982 and the Class of 1992. The inverse to this pattern can be observed for the proportions of grades that were "B" and "D." In terms of final undergraduate GPAs, those for women and students who earned bachelor's degrees, as well as among some majors (health sciences and services, social sciences, and applied social sciences), dropped from the Class of 1972 to the Class of 1982, then rose for the Class of 1992. [Adelman, 2004b, p. 77]*

It is worth noting that trend analysis of college grades could present different findings, depending on the data and the time frame used in the analysis. Although reported GPAs appear to fluctuate, a general pattern is apparent of grade increase on individual campuses and a qualifying upward trend of college grades for higher education as a whole.

Grade Inflation

Is grade inflation one of the causes for the increase in college grades? Because many factors can contribute to individual college grades and a variety of factors contribute to the change of institution-level grades over time, the problem of grade inflation must be examined from a multivariate perspective. Until now, only a handful of studies used the multivariate approach to analyze empirical data to unravel the college-grading puzzle.

Kuh and Hu (1999) used student self-reported grades in a CSEQ research program to examine the factors related to changes in student grades. Using complex statistical methods, Kuh and Hu analyzed self-reported grades of 22,792 students in the mid-1980s and 29,464 in the mid-1990s from 124 four-year colleges and universities. They argued that the increase of college grades over time is a complex combination of students' changing background, changing grade-awarding practices, and in some cases, artificial inflation of grades in colleges and universities (Hu and Kuh, 1998; Kuh and Hu, 1999). One intriguing feature of their study finds that the increase in college grades alone is not a valid indication of the artificial inflation of grades. In fact, average college grades can continue to increase even when artificial grade deflation does not occur on campus. Similarly, grade inflation might be at work even if average grades on campus are stable or even declining. Kuh and Hu's study (1999) also suggests that institutional type and college major serve as mediating factors in the phenomenon of grade increase.

Kuh and Hu's proposal on grade inflation was further tested by institution-level analysis. Wood, Ridley, and Summerville (1999) began their study on the premise that even if grades are leveled, a possibility remains of grade inflation, stemming from the logic advanced by Hu and Kuh (1998). Wood, Ridley, and Summerville used student GRE scores as the underlying criteria to test grade inflation. Their results suggest that grade inflation may or may not be occurring, depending on the criteria used. For instance, they found grade inflation related to combined GRE scores and GRE verbal scores, but not to GRE analytical scores and GRE quantitative scores. In addition, they found grade inflation to be more prevalent in "humanistic" rather than "scientific" fields.

Using student records in the registrar's office at Indiana University, Jacobs, Johnson, and Keene (1978) identified 261 courses taught by the same professors during two academic years (1970–71 and 1975–76). They separated the analyses for small and large classes (enrollment of fifty students as the cutoff point). SAT scores were included to control for the possible effect of students' changing academic ability. They found that "there was a significant increase in the average grades awarded in the same courses by the same professors after an adjustment was made for the ability levels of the students" (p. 9). The study identified student grades to be significantly higher in the selected 1975–76 classes despite the fact that average student SAT scores were significantly lower. In addition, they found that "the adjusted average grades in the small classes were found to be significantly higher than those of the large classes. Increase in adjusted average grades was somewhat greater for the small classes between the two years" (p. 6).

Mullen (1995) studied 23,064 full-time, first-time, first-year students at a university system from 1987 to 1992. Although the average system-wide GPA increased from 2.67 to 2.76 during this time, Mullen suggested that the increase in GPA could be explained by the increase in students' ACT composite scores from 24.39 to 25.27 and the corresponding increase in high school percentile ranks from 75.24 to 80.56. Olsen (1997) reached a similar conclusion after analyzing student records at Brigham Young University from 1975 to 1994. Both the change in student composition and the increased preparation of students (entering first-year students rose from the seventieth percentile in 1975 to the ninetieth percentile in 1994) were cited as the causes for the increase in student GPAs. Similarly, Hanson (1998) analyzed student GPA and SAT data at the University of Texas at Austin. He found that student GPAs increased from 1986 to 1995; however, student SATs appeared to have an even sharper increase during the same time period. He concluded that "given the 'quality' of the students, students [in 1995] earned lower grades, on average, than they would have in 1986."

McSpirit and Jones (1999) analyzed data of student grades from 1983 to 1996 at a large, open-admissions public university by controlling for the changes in student ACT scores, gender, major, and program. Their results indicated the existence of an inflationary trend in students' graduation GPAs when measured by college entry year, which also was a significant positive predictor of GPA. Further, their results suggest that lower-ability students experienced the highest rate of grade increase. Bejar and Blew (1981) used data from the College Board to examine the trend of student GPAs and SAT scores from 1964 to 1978. They found that college grades increased from 1964 to 1974 and then leveled off but that SAT scores were relatively stable over time, although fluctuations existed. They concluded that grade inflation was present from 1964 to 1974, because the increase in college grades was not accompanied by an increase in SAT scores.

Prather, Smith, and Kodras's study (1979) is perhaps one of the most enlightening studies on the college grading problem. They carefully differentiated grading patterns for individual courses and changes in student GPAs. Their findings suggest that "there is not a general, systematic increase in average grades throughout the 144 courses when controlling for student ability level and program of study" (p. 20). They found that different courses followed different grading patterns. Some courses emphasized quantitative and factual learning and were relatively low-grade areas, while career-oriented courses demonstrated high-grade patterns. Courses that showed a systematic increase over the five-year period often remained the lowest, even after taking the increase into account. A few high-grade courses decreased systematically over time. Thus, both the extremely high- and extremely low-grade courses demonstrated a trend of regressing toward the mean, while the majority of the courses (that is, the middle-grade courses) did not increase systematically from year to year for the five-year period studied. The longitudinal pattern, however, indicated that the percentage of students with final grades of A's increased, while those whose final grades were C's decreased. Not surprisingly, average GPAs increased dramatically at the university over this same period. Prather, Smith, and Kodras (1979) further suggest that university faculty generally did not change grading patterns in individual courses but that the changing course enrollment patterns coupled with disparities in grading across major fields drove up average final grades. They concluded that "many students involved in this shift have been exercising their prerogative of choice in order to avoid courses with traditionally low grading practices, resulting in course proliferation and increasing GPAs" (pp. 22–23). They developed a conceptual schema to illustrate how student GPA was influenced by their course choices (Figure 6).

Although the evidence suggests grade increase over time, empirical support of grade inflation is less than robust. Findings on grade inflation are more tentative and time and context sensitive. Nevertheless, grade inflation is a problem on some campuses and within certain types of institutions in a given historical time period (Hu and Kuh, 1998; Jacobs, Johnson, and Keene, 1978; Kuh and Hu, 1999; McSpirit and Jones, 1999).

FIGURE 6
A Conceptual Schema for Student GPAs

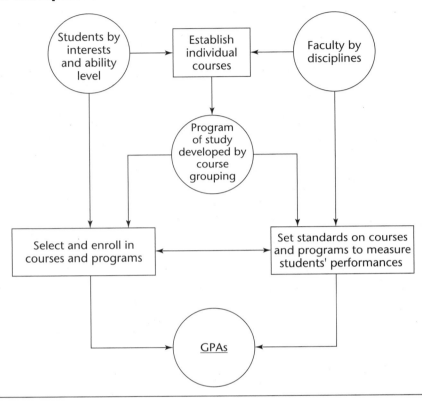

SOURCE: Prather, Smith, and Kodras, 1979, with minor modification.

Grade Compression

Critics of college grading practices worry that the inability of grades to differentiate students' performance may increase as college grades continue to rise. This phenomenon is known as grade compression (Hu and Kuh, 1998; Kuh and Hu, 1999; Rosovsky and Hartley, 2002). Mansfield (2001) argues forcefully that "grade inflation compresses all grades at the top, making it difficult to discriminate the best from the very good, the very good from the good, the good from the mediocre" (p. B24).

Although this argument is intuitively appealing, many disagree on this logic. Becker (1995) argues that even if average grades have increased, the phenomenon of grade inflation is "grossly exaggerated" (p. xiii) in that grades still have a nontrivial influence on the amount of effort students allocate to their studies. The grade inflation problem has not yet affected the reliability of grades, because grades do distinguish students in terms of academic efforts and performance (Ellenberg, 2002; Millman, Slovacek, Kulick, and Mitchell, 1983; Singleton and Smith, 1978). In Kuh and Hu's study (1999), students' efforts in educationally purposeful activities were consistently rewarded through the bestowing of higher grades. Ellenberg (2002) illustrated that as long as variations exist within college grades, even if the average grades increase, grades will continue to differentiate students properly. This argument is consistent with the research evidence found in other studies (Millman, Slovacek, Kulick, and Mitchell, 1983; Singleton and Smith, 1978).

Concerned that the increase in college grades might decrease the predictive power of the SAT and ACT, Breland (1976) examined the relationship between college GPAs on students' academic ability. The results indicate that college grades on average have increased. Concurrently occurring was a decrease in the traditional kinds of academic skills of the college-bound population. Yet the relationship between these skills and grades did not change. Breland concluded that "despite the increase in average grades, the reliability of the grades awarded by college professors has not diminished" (1976, p. 15).

Bejar and Blew (1981) found a similar conclusion in their studies examining the relationship between college grades and SAT scores. Even though they found that college grades increased without a corresponding increase in student SAT scores, the relationship between college grades and SAT scores was stable and even increased from 1964 to 1978.

"If grade inflation is viewed as the addition of a constant to grades it will not affect validity because the addition of such a constant would not affect the correlation of GPA and SAT. Beyond a point, however, the variability of GPA might be restricted causing a reduction in the correlation of GPA and SAT. The data presented do not suggest that point has been reached" (Bejar and Blew, 1981, p. 155).

Apparently, the arguments over the differentiating function of grades are hinged on conceptual distinctions among grade increase, grade inflation, and grade compression. Until now, the empirical evidence suggests that the increase in average college grades has not yet reached the point that the relation between grades and the underlying meritorious measures has diminished. Strong empirical evidence of grade compression does not exist; however, if college grades continue to rise, grades may lose their reliability as a result of grade compression.

The function of grades to differentiate students is but one of the many functions of grades. Even though the differentiating function of grades has yet to occur, the other functions of grades may suffer negative consequences. Kuh and Hu (1999) suggest that student cultures have established a normative academic effort threshold in response to the grading reward structure over time, noting that "many students learn that they can obtain a desirable grade by expending a certain amount of effort and put forth the least amount that produces the desirable grade" (Kuh and Hu, 1999, p. 318). This observation is consistent with Becker's reasoning (1982) that high-ability students may take grade inflation as a disincentive in the learning process.

Grading Disparity

Research has documented the existence of different grading policies and practices in different courses, departments, and academic disciplines. Sabot and Wakeman-Linn (1991) analyzed the disparity in grading practices in various departments. They found that student grade averages were lower in economics, chemistry, and mathematics than in art, English, music, philosophy, psychology, and political science. The existence of different practices in grading has raised concerns in the academic community. Regarding the issue of grade inflation in higher education, Mitchell (1998) argued that "far worse is the problem of grade variation within and among individual courses, which is camouflaged by the bold averages conveyed by news accounts" (p. A72). Empirical evidence shows the wide disparities in college grades among different courses and in different disciplines.

Researchers have examined grading disparity through the pair-wise comparison of grades received by the same students in courses from different departments. This treatment largely controlled for the confounding effects of individual student characteristics such as academic ability. Using this method, Goldman and Widawski (1976) found that major fields in science such as physics, chemistry, and biology awarded lower grades, while fields such as sociology, ethnic studies, and art tended to award higher grades. Synthesis on pair-wise studies indicates a pattern of grading disparities in college.

"There is a consistent trend for humanities departments to grade leniently . . . , for social sciences departments to grade in an approximately neutral manner, and for natural sciences and mathematics department to grade stringently. The notable exceptions to this trend are economics courses, where grading tends to be quite stringent, and sociology courses, where grading tends to be lenient" (Johnson, 2003, p. 205).

College grades are closely related to an array of factors such as student background, institutional characteristics, student academic preparation, and effort. The simple increase or decrease of average grades or shifts in grade distribution does not indicate grade inflation or deflation. The focus should be less on grades and more on the grading practice—the way that grades are assessed and awarded in individual courses.

Recent national empirical studies on college grading practices (Table 3), with the exception of Kuh and Hu's study (1999), examine the distribution of grades or changes in average grades over time (Adelman, 1999b; Horn, Peter, Rooney, and Malizio, 2002; Levine and Cureton, 1998; Rojstaczer, 2003). A slight inconsistency exists in the findings concerning the overall pattern of college grades. Although other studies confirm the increase of college grades over time, Adelman's study (2004b) shows the fluctuation of aggregated college grades when only a few time points are used. A study of grades throughout the whole time period would improve the accuracy of the overall longitudinal trend of college grades. Unfortunately, the NCES surveys students only periodically. It is important to note that these types of studies cannot confirm the existence of grade inflation. Further, using analytical methods without controlling for confounding factors is not conceptually strong, because the reasonable rival explanations are not eliminated.

TABLE 3
Summary of Recent Studies on College Grades

Study	Study Type	Years Studied	Publication Type	Student Input Measures	Method	Major Findings
1. Adelman (1999a)	National	1972–84, 1981–93	Report	No	Distribution of grades and average grades	Distribution of college grades was stable and average grades declined slightly
2. Horn, Peter, Rooney, and Malizio (2002)	National	1999–2000	Report	No	Distribution of grades	Large percentages of students received grade C or below
3. Kuh and Hu (1999)	National	1984–87, 1995–97	Journal article	Student effort	Multivariate analysis	Average grades increased across the board; grades inflated in some major fields and institutional types but deflated in others
4. Levine and Cureton (1998)	National	1967, 1976, 1993	Book	No	Distribution of grades	Percentages of students who received A's and B's increased while those who received C's or below decreased over time

Study	Level	Years	Document type	Test/control	Method	Findings
5. McSpirit and Jones (1999)	Institutional	1983–1996	Journal article	ACT	Multivariate analysis	Grade inflation appears to be more severe among lower-ability students
6. Mullen (1995)	Institutional	1987–1992	Conference paper	ACT and ranking	Multivariate analysis	Increase in average grades was result of change in student population
7. Olsen (1997)	Institutional	1975–1994	Conference paper	ACT and ranking	Multivariate analysis	Increase of average grades was result of change in student population
8. Rojstaczer (2003)	National	1968–2001	Report	No	Average grades	Average grades increased over time
9. Wood, Ridley, and Summerville (1999)	Institutional	1976–1980, 1984–1988, 1992–1996	Conference paper	GRE and its components	Multivariate analysis	Depending on the standard used, grade inflation may or may not have taken place

Institutional studies, on the other hand, can consider rival explanations. Interestingly, grade inflation is not strongly supported in many institution-specific studies. For example, both Mullen (1995) and Olsen (1997) argue that the increase in students' academic preparation primarily accounted for the increase in students' grades at two different universities. Institutions often are not willing to divulge the grade inflation problem, although an institution-specific study by McSpirit and Jones (1999) reports grade inflation at one university. Still, one needs to consider the potential sampling problem in research syntheses on grade inflation studies using institutional data sets.

Finally, as important as it is to consider the underlying meritorious-oriented measures when discussing the grade inflation problem, it is likewise necessary to determine and clarify the time period researched. Unfortunately, research on grade inflation seldom refers to the same time period and rarely uses the same reference time point, which often contributes to the production of conflicting research results. More troubling, the disagreement is heightened through data analysis. Some researchers use longitudinal data from a relatively long, consecutive time period (see, for example, Astin, 1997), while others choose a few time periods and compare the differences (Adelman, 1999b, for example). No serious distinction about long-term trends and short-term fluctuations can exist in any longitudinal event. Choosing two time periods to compare is subject to the problem of yearly grade fluctuations, a threat to the reliability of long-term projections. The comparison of grades in two time periods (or two cohorts) can be informative but may not be an accurate indication of a long-term trend.

In sum, empirical evidence from existing literature was reanalyzed with the guidance of the proposed framework. College grades have risen over time on many individual campuses, although this upward trend is less pronounced in nationwide studies. Most of the increase in college grades appears to be the result of factors other than grade inflation. In fact, no systematic evidence supports the assertion that grade inflation is widespread. Grade inflation appears to be a moderate problem at best. Grading disparity, on the other hand, is a serious threat to the integrity of college grading. It not only affects students' choice of courses but also provides incentives for faculty to lower their grading standards. Ironically, grading disparities more likely allow for grades in the less inflated courses to inflate, either because of the increasing pressure placed on professors or the fact that room remains for grade inflation. Currently, grade inflation and overall grade increases have not produced grade compression. Yet if grades continue to rise, grade compression is expected.

Uncovering the Roots

SHIFTS IN THE social, cultural, and political environments can affect the overall pattern of changes in college grades. Events such as the Vietnam War, the civil rights movement, and expanded postsecondary educational opportunities contribute to the changes in American higher education (Birnbaum, 1977; Goldman, 1985; Rosovsky and Hartley, 2002). These social forces influence colleges and universities directly and indirectly. As Birnbaum (1977) stated, "The factors operating within the campus environment [that] have been postulated to have affected grade point average cannot therefore be viewed in isolation, but must be considered in the context of a larger stage upon which the university was only one of a multiplicity of actors" (p. 524). College grades are related to a variety of factors and their interactions over time.

The grading problem is a set of intertwined problems. The interrelations of these problems are delineated in the guiding conceptual framework. The empirical evidence reviewed in this report suggests that it is important to focus on course grading practices to understand the changing pattern of GPAs, for both the individual students and for institutional averages. Colleges and universities have little or no control over the social environment within and surrounding the school. Therefore, one needs to focus on the grading problems that can be influenced by institutions' policies and practices.

Two grading problems emerge from the analysis. First, the grading disparity among different courses is the primary problem that contributes to the increase in individual student GPAs and institution-level average GPAs. Second, grade inflation within individual courses also contributes to grade increases. This section explores the causes for grade inflation and grading disparity and suggests helpful policies and programs that can be implemented to address these problems.

Influences on Grade Change

College grades are increasing on many campuses. Grades are related to a number of factors: the student, faculty, course, discipline, and institution. The main influences contributing to this upward trend are the changes in student population, grading disparity between courses, the shifting of students' course-taking patterns, and, to some extent, grade inflation.

Changing Students

Student characteristics, academic ability, and behaviors in college influence individual grades. It is important to investigate how students have changed over time to accurately understand why college grades have changed. College enrollment has expanded dramatically. Student enrollment in college sharply increased in the 1960s and 1970s. Since the late 1970s, total enrollment in college has continued to grow, from slightly more than twelve million in 1980 to more than fifteen million in 2000, representing more than a 25 percent increase in twenty years. More revealing is the change in enrollment rates by students of different characteristics (Table 4). The percentage of male students dropped from 48.5 percent in 1980 to 43.9 percent in 2000, while the percentage of female students increased from 51.5 percent to 56.1 percent. Given that female students typically receive higher grades in college than men, it is not surprising that this gender shift in enrollment has led to higher average college grades.

The racial and ethnic composition of college students also changed from 1980 to 2000, a trend that reflects the overall population change in American society. All minority groups increased their representation on college campuses, while the proportion of white students declined steadily over time. In a twenty-year span, the representation of white students dropped from 81.4 percent to 68.3 percent, and the percentage of American Indians increased from 0.7 percent to 1.0 percent. Asian enrollments increased from 2.4 percent to 6.4 percent,

TABLE 4
College Enrollment in Selected Years

		1980	1990	1995	1998	1999	2000
Total Number		12,086,800	13,818,600	14,261,800	14,507,000	14,791,200	15,312,300
Men	N	5,868,100	6,283,900	6,342,500	6,369,300	6,490,600	6,721,800
	%	48.50	45.50	44.50	43.90	43.90	43.90
Women	N	6,218,700	7,534,700	7,919,200	8,137,700	8,300,600	8,590,500
	%	51.50	54.50	55.50	56.10	56.10	56.10
American Indian	N	83,900	102,800	131,300	144,200	145,500	151,200
	%	0.70	0.70	0.90	1.00	1.00	1.00
Asian	N	286,400	572,400	797,400	900,500	913,000	978,200
	%	2.40	4.10	5.60	6.20	6.20	6.40
Black	N	1,106,800	1,247,000	1,473,700	1,582,900	1,643,200	1,730,300
	%	9.20	9.00	10.30	10.90	11.10	11.30
Hispanic	N	471,700	782,400	1,093,800	1,257,100	1,319,100	1,461,800
	%	3.90	5.70	7.70	8.70	8.90	9.50
White	N	9,833,000	10,722,500	10,311,200	10,178,800	10,282,100	10,462,100
	%	81.40	77.60	72.30	70.20	69.50	68.30

SOURCE: Chronicle of Higher Education, 2003.

African American enrollments from 9.2 percent to 11.3 percent, and Hispanic enrollments from 3.9 percent to 9.5 percent. This demographic change in the college student population has implications for college grades. The increasing representation of minority students impacts average grades, given that minority students in general receive lower grades in college. Another important factor related to college grades is students' academic ability and preparation. Traditionally, scores on the SAT and ACT were considered measures of students' academic ability. High school grades were also considered to be related to students' academic preparation. Because concerns surround grade inflation in high school (Goldman, 1985), it is appropriate to use standardized test scores as a baseline measure. Compiling data from the American College Testing program, Boesel and Fredland (1999) found that the ACT composite scores of freshmen dropped between 1970 and 1980, a continued trend of a general decline observed in different achievement tests in the late 1960s and 1970s. ACT scores rebounded in the 1980s and then exceeded the levels of the early 1970s by the mid-1990s (Figure 7). Boesel and Fredland's trend analysis on ACT scores considered the change in the test in 1989 and was converted to comparable measures. They concluded that "even though enrollments have increased greatly, college students today are at least as able as they were four decades ago" (Boesel and Fredland, 1999, p. 10). Data from the ACT program also indicated a steady upward trend of ACT scores into the 1990s (Figure 8). Given the positive correlation between ACT scores and student college GPAs, this rise in ACT scores may translate into increases in students' college grades, controlling for other factors.

Goldman (1985) hypothesized that the distribution of students in various institutions may have changed as college enrollments increased. The elite colleges may have become more selective, thus resulting in overall higher academic abilities of students enrolled in their institutions. Without the modification of grading standards, the average grades of the elite colleges would increase. This reasoning appears to be congruent with the rapid rise in college grades in elite institutions.

Another important factor related to college grades is student behavior in college. Research has unequivocally demonstrated that the most important factor in student learning during college is student engagement, or the quality of effort students devote to educationally purposeful activities that contribute

FIGURE 7
Trends in ACT Composite Scores of College Freshmen
from 1971 to 1994

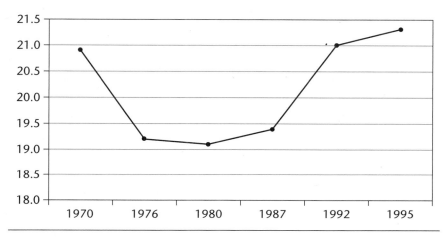

SOURCE: Boesel and Fredland, 1999.

FIGURE 8
Trends in ACT Composite Scores of ACT Takers
from 1991 to 2000

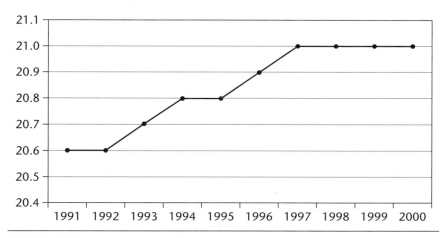

SOURCE: ACT Newsroom Report, multiple years.

directly to desired outcomes (Astin, 1993; Chickering and Reisser, 1993; Kuh, Schuh, Whitt, and associates, 1991; Pascarella and Terenzini, 1991). Higher education researchers have spent considerable time documenting student engagement. The evidence gained from national survey programs such as CSEQ and the National Survey of Student Engagement (NSSE) does not provide agreeable news for educators. Recent studies suggest that large numbers of college students appear to be academically or socially disengaged or both (Flacks and Thomas, 1998; Kuh, Hu, and Vesper, 2000). Survey evidence also suggests that student engagement has trended downward over time (Kuh, 1999; Young, 2002). Kuh (1999) compared the effort in educationally purposeful activities by two cohorts from different decades (the 1980s and the 1990s) and found a pattern of diminished effort among the 1990s cohort. The percentage of students devoting at least 40 hours a week to their studies dropped an average of 7 percent from the 1980s to the 1990s. The pattern of diminished effort is also evident on many other CSEQ survey items, including both academic and social activities (Kuh, 1999; Kuh and Hu, 1999). This downward trend in student engagement may lead to lower student grades.

In addition, educational aspiration for graduate education appears to be increasing among high school and college students, based on national surveys of high school seniors. Data from nationally representative samples of high school seniors indicate that the percentages of high school seniors who expect to continue their education with graduate school were 12.6 percent in 1972, 20.5 percent in 1980, and 33.3 percent in 1992, a dramatic increase in expectations over time (Boesel and Fredland, 1999, p. 5). The higher level of aspiration for graduate education could lead to better college grades for those aspiring students.

As summarized in Table 5, changes in student characteristics interact and affect student GPAs in complex ways. To understand the reasons that college-level grades change over time, one cannot ignore the historical development of American higher education and the demographical shift.

Grading Disparity and Student Course-Taking Patterns

After a course-by-course analysis of student grades at one university, Prather, Smith, and Kodras (1979) found that the change in students' course-taking

TABLE 5
Changes in Selected Student Characteristics and Potential Influences on Average College Grades

Characteristic	Change	Relation with Grades	Direction of the Influence on Average Grades
Women	⇑	+	⇑
Minorities	⇑	−	⇓
ACT	⇑	+	⇑
Quality of Effort	⇓	+	⇓
Degree Aspiration	⇑	+	⇑

patterns is responsible for changes in student GPAs. Although students may choose courses that they enjoy, in many cases changes in students' course-taking patterns are the result of changes in institutional policies and program requirements. They found that many academically rigorous core requirements were discarded and replaced by field-centered or experience-oriented courses. Because grades in those courses tend to be higher, student enrollment increased and average grades rose (Prather, Smith, and Kodras, 1979).

Course-taking patterns contain instances of change and stability. Adelman (1995b) estimates that about a third of entering students in the 1990s enrolled in at least one developmental academic skills course during their undergraduate program, a much larger fraction than in previous decades. This change could partially explain higher grades in the 1990s. In a recent study based on student transcripts, Adelman (2004a) found the following course-taking patterns by three cohorts (1972–1980, 1982–1990, and 1992–2000):

- Increasing proportions of students took courses in international management, management information systems, public speaking, aerobics/ jogging/body building, and ethics.
- Decreasing proportions of students took courses in education from 1972–1980 to 1982–1990, which rebounded in 1992–2000.
- Increasing proportions of students took courses in education from 1972–1980 to 1982–1990, which decreased in 1992–2000.

This changing course-taking pattern may not necessarily affect individual course grading, but it can influence both student and institution-level average GPAs as a result of the disparities in grading practices across courses and disciplines.

As more states implement merit-based financial aid, increased concerns have arisen over students' choosing courses with lenient grading practices as well as enrolling in fewer numbers of courses per semester (Sloop, 2000) to sustain qualifying grades for financial aid.

Grade Inflation

Any grade increase that cannot be accounted for by changes in student characteristics could be considered grade inflation. Explicit grade inflation occurs when a professor awards higher grades to different cohorts for work of similar quality. This type of grade inflation is moderately supported through research. Other forms of grade inflation are more implicit. Faculty characteristics affect grading practices. The change in faculty population over time may alter student grades. As Goldman (1985) suggests, "It seems likely that as older professors have retired from teaching, younger professors with more lenient grading practices have replaced them. Grade inflation could thereby occur even if the standards of all individual professors remained constant" (p. 102). This interpretation is plausible, given the increase in adjunct faculty. Research has shown that adjunct faculty members tend to award higher grades to students than regular faculty. Schuster and Finkelstein (forthcoming) completed a longitudinal analysis on the growth of the American faculty during the past four decades. The data compiled indicate a large growth in the number of both full-time and part-time faculty; however, the increase in part-time faculty members rose much faster than that for full-time faculty, resulting in a changing ratio of part-time to full-time faculty members from .28 in 1960 to .80 in 2001 (Table 6). This transformation of the American faculty is almost certain to drive up grades, barring any changes in grading patterns by faculty.

Changes in administrative practices regarding grades could be another implicit form of grade inflation as colleges and universities have adopted more liberal policies governing grading. For instance, various types of grades used to affect student grades negatively but are now treated as nonpenalty grades.

TABLE 6
Growth of the American Faculty by Employment Status,
Selected Years 1970–2001 (Numbers in Thousands)

Year	All	% Change	Full-time	% Change	Part-time	% Change	Part/Full Ratio
1970	474	—	369	—	104	—	0.28
1975	628	32.5	440	8.4	188	16.8	0.43
1980	686	9.2	450	1.1	236	2.6	0.52
1985	715	4.2	459	−0.7	256	0.4	0.56
1991	826	15.5	536	2.3	291	−3.0	0.54
1993	915	10.8	546	1.9	370	27.2	0.68
1995	932	1.9	551	0.9	381	3.0	0.69
1997	990	6.2	569	3.3	421	10.5	0.74
1999	1,028	3.8	591	3.9	437	3.8	0.74
2001	1,113	8.3	618	4.6	495	13.3	0.80
% Change							
1970–2001		134.8		67.5		376.0	
1980–2001		62.2		37.3		109.7	
1991–2001		34.7		15.3		70.1	

SOURCE: Schuster and Finkelstein (forthcoming).

This category includes, but is not limited to, late withdrawal provisions, removal of first-attempt grades from transcripts if students later repeat the course and earn a higher grade, and pass-fail or credit–no credit grades. In fact, Adelman (2004b) discovered that the changes in grading practices from the 1970s through the 1990s were the growing proportion of withdrawals and no-credit repeats.

Causes of Grading Disparity

Grades are the only tangible reward students receive in college (Bean, 1985), and students respond to these incentives through their choice of courses (Sabot and Wakeman-Linn, 1991). After investigating the influence of student course choices in a college, Sabot and Wakeman-Linn (1991) found that the effect of student grades received in the first course impacted the probability of enrollment in the second course. This outcome was particularly true in the departments of economics, English, and mathematics and less evident in political science and psychology. Johnson (2003) found similar results using data from undergraduate students at Duke University; students were not motivated to take courses in the lower-grading fields if they were not required. This effect could distort students' choice of courses if large disparities in grading practices exist among different disciplines.

Freeman (1999) offered an explanation of the disparity in grading practices among different fields. He suggested that "given equal money prices per credit hour across disciplines, departments manage their enrollments by 'pricing' their courses with grading standards commensurate with the market benefits of their courses, as measured by expected incomes" (p. 344). Results from his study using NCES data confirm that fields associated with higher starting salaries had lower GPAs than those associated with greater "income risk" (p. 350). One implication could be that the departments manage student enrollment through the manipulation of grading practices. Other researchers suggest that enrollment pressures and fiscal policies are responsible (Stone, 1995). Goldman, Schmidt, Hewitt, and Fisher (1974) found that fields with lower-ability students tend to adopt lower grading standards, while higher standards are implemented in fields with higher-ability students. Further, courses with lenient grading standards tend to have growth in student enrollment. Given that faculty hiring is largely based on course enrollment, it can be assumed that an incentive exists for departments to adopt more lenient grading practices (Goldman and Hewitt, 1975).

Broski (1998) offers another interpretation focusing on the causes of grading disparities among disciplines. He argues that grading is a costly procedure because it demands that faculty members spend considerable time to accurately evaluate students' academic performance. Further, these grading costs differ across disciplines. Evaluations of students' work in the social sciences and humanities tend to be more subjective than in science and engineering. Faculty members in the social sciences and humanities would have to spend more time defending their grading if they were to adopt stringent grading policies, which would increase grading costs and result in the likelihood of faculty members' adopting lenient grading practices.

Therefore, grading disparity provides incentives for various participants at colleges and universities. Students are attracted to courses with lower grading standards, particularly when merit-based financial aid programs are associated with college grades. Academic departments are motivated to offer courses with lenient grading practices to boost student enrollments, which also translates into financial advantage for the university. Universities need to eliminate these incentives to stop the practice of grading disparity.

Further, grading disparity between courses also promotes grade inflation, particularly for courses that traditionally award lower grades. Shea's report (1994) in *The Chronicle of Higher Education* justified this concern. Shea reported that faculty members in the lower-grading departments became more aware of grading disparity among different disciplines. They thought that they might have to inflate their grades to compete with other courses for student enrollment. Sabot, one of the authors who published research on grading disparity and grade inflation (Sabot and Wakeman-Linn, 1991), admitted that mathematics and science professors, who traditionally bestow lower grades, have an incentive to become more lenient with grades when they recognize grading disparities. Sabot stated that their intent was to restrain grade inflation, but in reality the opposite happened (Shea, 1994).

Causes of Grade Inflation

Scholars and researchers have offered multiple explanations for the phenomenon of grade inflation. Student evaluation of teaching, the "disengagement compact" between student and faculty, and merit-based financial aid are the potential causes attracting the most attention.

Student Evaluation of Teaching

Among all the suggested causes, student evaluation of teaching has become one of the primary reasons for grade inflation in colleges (Centra, 2003; Eiszler, 2002; Johnson, 2003; Marsh and Roche, 2000). Arguments claim that the use of student evaluation of teaching in faculty personnel decisions pushed faculty to grade leniently in the hope of receiving favorable student evaluations (see Marsh and Roche, 2000).

The unintended consequence of student evaluation of teaching on grade inflation has attracted considerable research interest. Extensive research has looked into the relationship between grades and student evaluations of teaching. Directly related to the topic of college grading problems are two issues. The first issue centers on the factual aspects of the relationship, or whether there exists a positive or negative association between grades and student evaluation of teaching. The second issue focuses on the interpretative aspects of the relationship, or the meaning of a positive or negative relationship. In fact, this seemingly straightforward research topic has plagued researchers for decades and still continues (Centra, 2003; Eiszler, 2002; Johnson, 2003; Krautmann and Sander, 1999).

Johnson (2003) studied the relationship between grades and student evaluation of teaching and examined the contrasting interpretations. He concluded that "nearly all studies conducted have resulted in reports of a positive correlation between these variables, but debate continues over the cause of this association" (p. 47). The central issue of the research is whether student evaluation of teaching causes the awarding of higher grades. Critics of grade inflation tend to believe in the grade-leniency theory, which suggests that teachers give out higher grades to "buy" good student evaluations. On the other hand, proponents for the teacher-effectiveness theory argue that students learn more in courses offered by more effective teachers. This theory suggests that both high student evaluations of teaching and high grades are related to the instructor's teaching effectiveness. As Johnson reasoned, "If correlations between grades and student evaluations of teaching result from differences in teacher effectiveness, then corrections to teacher-course evaluations for differences in the assigned grades are both unnecessary and inappropriate. If, on the other hand, positive correlations between student grades and student evaluation of teaching are explained by student attribution or grade-leniency effects, corrections to teacher-course evaluations are needed to avoid the repercussion" (pp. 73–75). Johnson conducted the Duke Undergraduates Evaluate Teaching experiment. His results demonstrate that the effects are both substantively and statistically important and suggest that "instructors can often double their odds of receiving high evaluations from students simply by awarding A's rather than B's or C's" (p. 83).

A recently published study by Centra (2003) argues otherwise. Centra investigated whether average grades influenced student ratings of instructors. Centra found that expected grades generally did not affect student evaluations. He further argues that professors of courses in the natural sciences with students expecting grades of A were rated lower, not higher. Eiszler (2002) found a positive and strong relationship between expected grades and the percentage of students reporting a likely grade of A or A– and teacher rating, controlling for the effects of prior achievement, the attractiveness of the courses, and the appeal of specific instructors. Eiszler (2002) further suggests that "in spite of the validity of ratings as indicators of teaching effectiveness in any given semester, it is possible to use them in ways that result in gradual grade inflation that only become apparent over the course of a decade or more" (p. 498).

Disengagement Compact

After analyzing national data collected by CSEQ on students' effort toward educationally purposeful activities and student self-reported college grades, Kuh (1999, 2003) offered his "disengagement compact" theory. This theory reflects the contemporary dynamics between college students and their teachers: "I'll leave you alone if you leave me alone." In essence, faculty members tend to not make students work too hard, yet they distribute high grades to reduce their time in grading student work as well as dealing with possible grading questions. Kuh discovered that many students received high grades, B's or better, even though they put forth relatively little effort. Kuh (2003) lamented that this "seems to be a breakdown of shared responsibility for learning—on the part of faculty members who allow students to get by with far less than maximal effort, and on the part of students who are not taking full advantage of the resources institutions provide" (p. 28). He suggests that both students and their teachers are responsible for this educational malaise. "Students are shortchanging themselves by not devoting as much effort to the activities that matter to their education as did their counterparts of a decade ago. Equally troubling, they are being shortchanged by their teachers. That is, it appears that faculty are contributing to the diminished-effort phenomenon by asking less from students in return for higher grades" (Kuh, 1999, p. 113).

The responsibility of the "disengagement compact" perhaps has much to do with graduate school socialization and institutional reward systems. The "publish or perish" mentality is deeply entrenched in the current tenure and promotion system. Faculty members often feel that they would be better served by devoting more time to research and less time to teaching and services. In response, faculty dole out higher grades to save time from having to communicate with students about assignments and defending their grading practices.

In essence, the "disengagement compact" theory is consistent with Broski's argument (1998) concerning grading costs. Grading is a costly process to faculty members (Broski, 1998). The more time faculty members spend in grading, the higher the costs to them. Under the current reward structure in academe, faculty members reduce their costs in grading while shifting more time toward research. Further, grade inflation is more severe in elite universities because faculty members feel more pressure to conduct research (Rosovsky and Hartley, 2002).

Merit-Based Financial Aid

State-sponsored merit-based financial aid is an interesting topic in higher education policy. One exemplary merit-based financial aid program is the HOPE scholarship program in the state of Georgia. To be eligible to receive this scholarship, students must maintain a decent cumulative GPA. Merit aid programs are politically popular, and currently a number of states have similar programs in place.

Critics of merit aid programs assert that providing financial aid contingent on student GPA will inevitably ensure the resurgence of grade inflation in college. In criticizing the HOPE scholarship's B grade point average requirement, Mortenson (1997) stated, "During the Vietnam War, some college professors were unwilling to give grades to males that would expose them to being drafted for military service. Noticeable grade inflation occurred then. Grade inflation is a rampant problem in high schools and colleges now. The incentives for faculty who care about their student's qualification for financial aid are to award qualifying grades" (p. 3). Sloop (2000) used data from the University System of Georgia to examine whether the HOPE scholarship resulted in grade inflation. She found an increase in first-year student grades after the implementation of the HOPE scholarship program. Although changing student characteristics and student preparation can explain the increase of first-year student grades, she concluded that grade inflation existed on certain campuses. Henry and Rubenstein (2002), on the other hand, suggest that the grade inflation problem did not occur with the adoption of the HOPE program. Their research examined the correlation between student grades and student achievement as evidenced by SAT scores. Therefore, what they found is in fact the nonexistence of grade compression instead of grade inflation as a result of the HOPE program.

It still remains to be seen whether state merit scholarship programs cause grade inflation and grade compression. Given the high-stakes environment produced by the merit aid scholarships, faculty members feel more pressure to grade leniently.

Incentive Matters

Grading disparity and grade inflation are the two primary problems in college grading. These problems have multiple causes, but inappropriate incentives for faculty members, students, and the academic departments are the main causes.

For students, grades are the most tangible rewards in college (Bean, 1985). Grades are indicators of students' academic achievement and accomplishment, they promote student self-esteem and sense of assurance, and they provide opportunities for students to further their education. College grades also have strong economic implications. Higher grades are found to have a significant and positive impact on students' entry into the labor market and their respective earnings (Pascarella and Terenzini, 1991). College students are eager to learn and develop themselves academically and personally. They are also focused on their grades (Becker, Geer, and Hughes, 1995; Milton, Pollio, and Eison, 1986). Obtaining satisfactory grades is a part of campus culture that will not likely change overnight (Kuh and Hu, 1999). The key issue for educators is whether the incentives are right for students. Grading disparity is an inappropriate incentive for students, for students often choose courses with lenient grading practices.

Inappropriate incentives embedded in the current system for faculty members are strong and even more alarming. These incentives contribute to both grading disparity and grade inflation. Tenure and promotion are important for faculty members in colleges and universities, but if lenient grading produces improved student evaluations of teaching, faculty are more likely to lower their grading standards. A related issue is faculty productivity. The long-standing debate surrounding scholarship appears to have achieved closure by the landmark work of Boyer (1990), which provides an enlarged perspective of scholarship (discovery, integration, application, and teaching). Yet faculty members recognize that excellence in research carries more weight than teaching and service. Lenient grading is an easy way for faculty to reduce costs in grading and teaching responsibilities and thus free time for research, a mechanism of disengaging (Kuh, 1999, 2003). In addition, the adoption and implementation of state merit-aid financial programs increase pressure to grade leniently.

Higher education institutions are considered unique organizations, and faculty members traditionally enjoy special social status. Yet both students and faculty members respond to both appropriate and inappropriate incentives. To solve these undesirable practices in college grading, higher education administrators need to find a mechanism to eliminate the undesirable incentives for both students and faculty.

In sum, multiple factors are related to the change of college grades. Some are beyond the direct control of institutions, and others can be affected by institutional policymakers. Changes in students' characteristics, which reflect overall trends in the American population, influence the patterns of college grades but are not subject to direct institutional policy interventions. Institutions can and should tackle the two main problems in grading—grading disparity and grade inflation. The move toward institutions' hiring more adjunct faculty, which contributes to grade inflation, needs to be examined and considered in institutional policy. The embedded incentives based on student enrollments deserve careful reconsideration so that improper incentives are eliminated. Academic policy regarding faculty performance evaluation appears to be a key component in the grading problem. Student evaluations of faculty teaching effectiveness and the constant emphasis on faculty research productivity reflect the academy's struggle in properly defining the measurement of scholarship (Boyer, 1990). Institutions need to redefine the evaluation of scholarship for their faculty to change the incentive structure so that faculty members can establish new priorities that can eliminate grading problems.

Searching for Cures

GRADING PROBLEMS in higher education are complex. To explore effective strategies to correct inappropriate grading practices, the higher education community needs to differentiate the distinct grading problems.

The grading problem must be understood from a multilevel perspective. Average institution-level GPA is a product of student characteristics and grading practices. Grade inflation, grading disparity, and their interaction have driven up individual student GPAs and institution-level college grades. Both the conceptual and empirical evidence supports this assessment. Grading disparity accounts primarily for the increase in student GPAs and institution-level average grades, as students have been choosing courses with higher average grades. Grade inflation is also a problem; however, the magnitude of grade inflation is not as substantial as grading disparity. These two types of problems need to be addressed for the good of higher education and society. "The problem is not only that most institutions have accepted grading practices that persistently blur the distinction between good and outstanding performance, while they award passing grades for showing up and turning in work—even when that work is poor. It is also that students and faculty members, administrators and trustees, accrediting bodies, and higher-education associations have been united for more than 25 years in their willingness to ignore, excuse, or compromise with grade inflation rather than fight it" (Kamber and Biggs, 2002, p. B14).

Emerging Practices

Exactly as Kamber and Biggs (2002) complained, higher education institutions are not particularly quick in dealing with various grading problems on campus. Although conversations about grading problems are abundant, actions aimed at addressing those problems are scarce. One of the most popular strategies used in higher education to counter grading problems is the expanded contextual transcript (Rosovsky and Hartley, 2002). Indiana University offers such a transcript: information on the transcript includes the context of the course, the instructor, and indexed grades from all students who took the class (Indiana University Office of the Registrar, 2004; Pugh, 2000). Student grades are indexed to reflect "the number of students in the course who received the same grade or higher compared to the total number of students in the section who received GPA grades" (Indiana University Office of the Registrar, 2004).

Further, information regarding grade distribution, class GPA, percentage of majors, and average student GPA for each section is reported on the transcript. The Web site for the registrar's office (2004) provides detailed information:

> *Grade Distribution shows the number of students in the course section receiving each of the possible grades that can be awarded. Class GPA is the average of all GPA grades awarded in the course section. It is calculated by totaling the credit points for all GPA grades awarded in the section and dividing by the total number of GPA grades. The Percentage of Majors is the percentage of students in the course section whose major school (or major department for the College of Arts and Sciences or University Graduate School students) matches the school or department offering the course. The Average Student GPA is calculated by averaging the record GPAs of all students enrolled in the course section at the time the grade context information is compiled. The GPA level used for each student is the student's GPA level (undergraduate or graduate). Grades awarded for the semester displayed are included in this calculation. [Indiana University Office of the Registrar, 2004]*

Recently, calls have increased for constraining course grade distributions as a way to contain grade inflation and as an approach to address grading disparity. Johnson (2003) claims that "carefully designed constraints on mean course grades provide the most comprehensive solution to problems associated with disparities in grading practices" (p. 243). Princeton University, for example, has proposed a reform plan in undergraduate grading by stipulating that students can achieve no more than 35 percent A's in regular courses and no more than 55 percent A's in junior and senior independent courses in a department (Hoover, 2004; see the appendix for the full proposal). The effectiveness of this type of policy in addressing grading problems in higher education remains to be seen.

Strategies and Innovations

Problems of grading disparity and grade inflation, explicit or implicit, need to be addressed so that grades better fulfill the functions of promoting student learning and providing trustworthy information for end users. In some cases, an overhaul of the current system may become necessary to make grades convey meaningful and useful information to various interested parties (Bressette, 2002; Rosovsky and Hartley, 2002).

Given the historical concerns about college grading problems, many researchers and scholars have proposed strategies to remedy existing problems. The negative effects of grading disparity have been the focus of several proposals. Examples include honors point scores, relative performance indexing, and achievement indexing. Honors point scores (de Nevers, 1984) take into consideration the individual student grade and class average grade in a formula to calculate the score. It is straightforward and simple but does not consider the competition found in different classes (de Nevers, 1984). The Relative Performance Index (RPI) also reflects student performance relative to the standard set by the faculty (Nagle, 1998), which is similar to the approach proposed by de Nevers. Achievement indexing (Johnson, 1997, 2003) is more sophisticated, as it is based on a complicated statistical computation. It was originally proposed by Johnson (1997) as an attempt to remedy grading disparity at Duke University. The basic intention is to adjust student GPA upward or downward based on the difficulty of the class as reflected by the distribution of student grades from the class. Although the essence of this type of adjustment is to eliminate certain incentives for students' choice of courses, it can also be integrated into faculty performance measures by adjusting student enrollment by the degree of the difficulty of the class.

More important, efforts need to be put forth to prevent grading problems. Broski (1998) suggests that the grading process in higher education has three roles: teaching, grading, and legislating. Institutions enact a general guideline on grading policies as a way of legislating. Various grading problems can be addressed in this institutional legislating process; however, the key to addressing many grading problems is the degree of separation between teaching and grading. When teaching and grading are totally separated, it is reasonable to expect that many problems such as grade inflation are less likely to occur. Broski (1998) cautioned, however, that this total separation could become a threat to faculty members' academic freedom, one of the core values in higher education. Nevertheless, this framework does offer insights in developing strategies to counter grading problems by searching for the optimal separation between teaching and grading. To effectively prevent problems in college grading, a concerted effort from all interested parties in the academic community is required.

A Shared Responsibility

All interested parties share the responsibility to address the issues surrounding college grading: accreditation bodies, state governments, boards of trustees, faculty, and students must solidify effective policies and practices in college grading.

Faculty are major participants in higher education governance, and academic policies often originate from the faculty. Their awareness of grading problems, willingness to address the problems, and competency in grading students fairly and rigorously all contribute to the restoration of good practices in college grading. It is shortsighted to think that the containment of grading problems is not in the interest of the faculty, as some critics point out (Johnson, 2003). Given the eroding public confidence in higher education, faculty members need to recognize that undesirable grading practices will damage the collective well-being of the academy. The academy must foster a culture of good practices in grading and adopt some technical strategies to correct current and future problems. Faculty senates and councils need to be proactive in starting the conversations about grading and actively pursue strategies to correct the problems. Rosovsky and Hartley (2002) suggest that colleges and universities should encourage institutional dialogue on college grading problems, given that systematic and constructive conversations on grading practices are rare. Further, many incoming faculty members are not familiar with their university's grading practices. Professors do not know how their grading practices compare with those of their colleagues and faculty from other departments. Open conversations about grading policies and the dissemination of information can enhance faculty members' willingness to adopt good practices in grading (Rosovsky and Hartley, 2002).

Higher education administrators, department chairs, deans, and chief academic officers can influence good grading practices. Yet individual faculty members or a single department cannot solve the problem of grading disparity. It requires systematic work throughout the whole institution. Stringent graders, who are likely to have lower course enrollments and lower student evaluations of teaching, are at risk of not receiving tenure, salary increases, or promotions (Johnson, 2003). Therefore, policies need to address this underlying incentive structure that inappropriately favors lenient grading. The use of student evaluations of teaching needs to be carefully assessed. Student evaluations of teaching must be prudently used and possibly incorporated into other measures of faculty teaching performance such as peer evaluations of teaching. The incentive structure that unintentionally encourages the "disengagement compact" needs to be reexamined and modified. Perhaps a careful measure of faculty out-of-class engagement with students can be considered in faculty teaching performance. Additionally, colleges and universities need to provide professional development and training opportunities for faculty on effective grading practices to increase faculty awareness and willingness to grade students fairly and vigorously (Walvoord and Anderson, 1998).

State policymakers can also help resolve grading problems in higher education. In states where merit aid programs are linked with college grades, policymakers need to recognize that this program configuration creates a context that could escalate the problems of grade inflation and grading disparity. Faculty members are reluctant to put students at financial risk through their distribution of lower grades. To keep their scholarships, students often adjust their programs of study and course choices to increase their GPAs. As a result, academic departments ease their grading standards to increase student enrollment. A carefully considered state financial aid program that does not rely on grade attainment can provide favorable outcomes for grading problems in higher education.

Policy Instruments as a Guide for Policy Design

Innovative ideas and exemplary practices alone are not sufficient for successful reform in college grading practices. Even policies with good intentions can go wrong (Fowler, 2000). An equally important aspect of effective policies is their successful implementation. Policy instruments can "translate substantive policy goals . . . into concrete actions" (McDonnell and Elmore, 1987, p. 134). The five policy instruments developed by McDonnell and her colleague are mandates, inducements, capacity building, system change, and hortatory policy (Fowler, 2000; McDonnell, 1994; McDonnell and Elmore, 1987).

A mandate is a "rule governing the actions of individuals and agencies" (McDonnell and Elmore, 1987, p. 138). The best context for effective mandates is uniform behavior along with strong supports. It takes the organization to enforce the mandates and the individuals to comply. Mandates however "usually create an adversarial relationship between the enforcing agency and those who do not wish to comply" (Fowler, 2000, p. 251). With respect to college grading problems, one must encourage uniform grading practices to eliminate grading disparities; however, given the considerable freedom faculty members traditionally enjoy in higher education, the opposition to mandates may be enormous. Administrators need to maintain strong leadership roles to communicate and persuade the faculty to reform their practices.

An inducement is a "transfer of money to individuals or agencies in return for the production of goods or services" (McDonnell and Elmore, 1987, p. 138). Because inducements are voluntary, some may respond to inducements and others may not. Therefore, inducements may not generate uniform behavior, but often they do not produce reactions as strong as mandates. Inducements for good grading practices can be considered as the first step toward systematic reform.

Capacity building is a mechanism defined as "the transfer of money to individuals or agencies for the purpose of investment in future benefits" (McDonnell and Elmore, 1987, p. 139). Capacity building as a policy instrument is suited for individuals or organizations that cannot perform to meet desirable expectations. It focuses on current participants' "lack of capacity." Higher education institutions may find capacity building a good investment in fighting grade inflation by providing their faculty members appropriate professional development opportunities (Walvoord and Anderson, 1998).

System change is "the transfer of official authority among individuals and agencies" (McDonnell and Elmore, 1987, p. 139). It addresses the issue of participants' "lack of willingness." System change has mostly taken place in graduate admissions. Increasing numbers of graduate schools rely less on students' undergraduate transcripts and more on standardized tests scores in making admissions decisions. "Once the professors have reduced their grades to an absurdity, and rendered that particular currency worthless, other units of account will necessarily spring up to take its place: recommendations from professors, 'personal essays', interviews, standardized tests—areas in which students from the most inflated universities happen to excel. The spur to competition will remain; the information will continue to flow. But watch out, faculty members: these alternative currencies sound as though they involve more work and trouble than simply giving true grades in the first place" (*The Economist,* 2002, p. 74).

Hortatory policy (or persuasion) sends "a signal that particular goals and actions are considered a high priority" (McDonnell, 1994, p. 398). It

TABLE 7
Policy Instruments for Different Participants in Grading Policy Design

| Participant | Instrument | | | | |
---	Mandates	Inducements	Capacity Building	System Change	Hortatory Policy
Accreditation Agency		Substitutes the requirement of external assessment of student learning with student grades, if student grades are demonstrated valid and reliable		Requires external assessment of student learning	
Board of Trustees				Overhauls existing grading policy and practice on campus	Advocate for rigorous and fair grading
Senior Institutional Administrators	Stipulate distribution in course grades so that grade inflation and grading disparity can be contained	Modify assessment of faculty teaching effectiveness	Provide faculty members the opportunity to attend workshops and training sessions on good practices in college grading		Initiate institutional dialogue and open conversations about grading problems on campus

	Hold academic deans and departmental chairs accountable for grading problems in their units	Adjust the use of student evaluations of teaching in promotion and tenure decisions	Advocate for rigorous and fair grading
		Reform resource allocation mechanisms among schools and colleges	Disseminate information of grade distribution in different colleges and academic departments
Midlevel Administrators		Enact reward policies for good grading practices as reflected in course grade distribution	Disseminate information about grade distribution in different courses
		Provide faculty members the opportunity to attend workshops and training sessions on good practices in college grading	Advocate for rigorous and fair grading
			Converse with faculty members whose course grading practices are problematic

(Continued)

TABLE 7 (Continued)
Policy Instruments for Different Participants in Grading Policy Design

| Participant | Instrument | | | | |
	Mandates	Inducements	Capacity Building	System Change	Hortatory Policy
Faculty Senate	Adjust student grades to address grading disparity across disciplinary boundaries Refine student transcript format to contextualize student course grades		Provide faculty members the opportunity to attend workshops and training sessions on good practices in college grading		Initiate institutional dialogue and open conversations on grading problems on campus Advocate for rigorous and fair grading Support faculty members who uphold rigorous and fair grading practices
Departmental Faculty	Adopt a self-imposed grading policy to ensure rigorous and fair grading				Discuss desirable grade distribution Advocate for rigorous and fair grading

emphasizes the role of information and symbols in changing individual behaviors. Given the organizational characteristics of higher education institutions, this policy instrument is particularly appealing to use. Grading problems are detrimental to the fulfillment of colleges' and universities' social and public missions. These costs often outweigh the benefits (Kezar, 2004). Faculty governing bodies and higher education administrators can create a climate of urgency in change and reform among all constituents. Addressing grading problems on campus swiftly and properly can enhance the collective well-being of the higher education community and the public good.

Different policy instruments are suitable in different contexts. Table 7 summarizes various policy instruments suitable for different participants in grading and policymaking. Although analytically separated, the five policy instruments can be used in combination to achieve optimal policy outcomes. In fact, it may be desirable to diversify and combine policy instruments in designing effective grading policies.

In sum, it takes some effort to convince those who are skeptical about grading problems in higher education. It takes even more effort for a whole campus community to eradicate various grading problems and restore the integrity of college grading. The incentive structure embedded in the current system encourages students to choose courses where they can receive high grades. Faculty members in turn become lenient graders, and departments become academic units that dispense high grades. Unfortunately, it is not in the interest of many on campus to change current grading practices. Technical strategies can help eliminate some incentives for students to choose high-grading courses and for faculty members to give out high grades. But to ultimately correct college grading problems, it takes a change in the campus culture. Administrators can use various policy instruments to achieve policy goals. It is the faculty, though, who can refresh the grading process and promote student learning. Eventually, this change will reclaim the public's confidence in college grades as indicators of student performance and learning.

Conclusions and Implications

CRITICS CONSISTENTLY ARGUE that many problems afflict current grading practices in American colleges and universities. College grades are on the rise over time despite occasional fluctuations—evident from the compilation of all college grades over the long term. Many factors are related to this upward trend in college grades. The changing student population is one of the most important factors that affect the average of college grades. Contrary to the critics' assertions, however, entering college students' academic abilities as measured by the ACT actually have not declined during the past two decades. Grade inflation might be occurring in colleges and universities, but it is not seen to be as severe as reflected in reports from the general press. Although the belief is widespread that the increase in college grades and grade inflation might diminish the differentiating function of college grades, no strong empirical evidence suggests that it is the case. Although grade compression has not become as severe a problem in college grading practices, grading practices in different courses, major fields, and disciplines are widely disparate. Under these circumstances, student enrollment patterns in coursework, by choice or by requirement, has contributed to the change in college grades.

College grading problems are complex. The discussion on the phenomenon must be institution and time specific and take into consideration the context of American higher education. Further, one needs to differentiate a steady pattern of grade inflation that might warrant policy interventions from the yearly fluctuation of college grades. Whenever college grading becomes a concern, it is important to first determine the specific problem and adopt appropriate corrective strategies.

Those who are concerned about the well-being of students and the betterment of higher education must understand the profound role of grades in the educational process. Used properly, the grading process can be a powerful tool in motivating students to learn and to improve the quality of faculty teaching (Walvoord and Anderson, 1998). Accordingly, a rigorous and fair grading process can produce reliable and useful information for the end users of college grades. A strong grading system can create a win-it-all situation for colleges and universities. Teaching and learning will be enhanced, the public trust in higher education institutions restored.

Implications for Research

Although debates abound on college grading problems in the press, surprisingly few empirical studies have been published in academic journals. Many conversations about grading problems are anecdotal and driven by opinion. To establish a robust knowledge base on college grading problems, empirical studies based on a sound conceptual framework and quality databases are needed.

The Value of the Conceptual Framework

The comprehensive framework for college grading problems provides a means to understand a multilevel and multifaceted problem in college grading. The distinction between grades, GPAs for individual students, and institutional averages informs researchers that there are multiple ways to operationalize outcome variables in empirical analyses. They all have different implications for what needs to be included as exploratory input variables. The results may lead to different policy actions. For example, in examining grade inflation, individual course grades are a better indicator than student GPAs, because GPAs are influenced by student course portfolios. When one is interested in explaining the change in institution-level average GPAs over time, it is necessary to consider the changes in student population to present an accurate account.

The differentiation of grading problems (grade change, grade inflation, grade compression, and grading disparity) and their interrelations clarify different aspects of college grading problems. Researchers then can clearly formulate what problems they are interested in and design their research accordingly. Even though grading disparity and grade inflation may be connected, they are two different types of problems and require different investigative methods. Similarly, grade inflation and grade compression, although linked in many cases, are different problems. Grade inflation in its extreme format can lead to grade compression, but it will not necessarily result in grade compression if there is room for grades to rise. Conversely, grade compression can be a problem with or without the problem of grade inflation. Grade compression can occur whenever grades are confined within a limited range without an adequate variation among grades.

The Need for Additional Research

This report provides conceptual evidence of grading problems in higher education. It also reviews empirical studies to provide concrete evidence about college grading. Most research in this area is not based on a clearly stated conceptual framework. In fact, no shared common ground guided these studies. It is clear that additional studies are needed to advance our understanding of an important problem in higher education. Specifically, empirical studies in the following directions are particularly useful.

First, course-based longitudinal studies will help clarify the changing nature of college grading practices. As long as grading disparities exist among different courses, researchers need to focus on course-based studies to understand whether grade inflation has taken place. Of course, the collection of student characteristics in different cohorts in the longitudinal study is important because these characteristics affect student grades.

Second, whenever a discernable problem of grade inflation arises, a set of explanations of the problem can be explored. For instance, longitudinal studies can help answer questions about whether grade inflation is the result of change in faculty characteristics, student evaluations of teaching, or institutional policy.

Third, grading disparity needs to be studied more thoroughly. Not only is it an important problem in itself, but it also has a lot in common with grade inflation. Many explanations of grading disparity exist, including the impact of the labor market, the differences in grading philosophies, the match between subject areas and student interest, and the differences in student abilities. Further analysis could help confirm or refute these interpretations.

Finally, it is necessary to conduct evaluative studies of various strategies proposed or adopted to counter grading problems. For instance, different strategies to adjust grading disparity have been proposed, but how effective they are in achieving policy goals is still unclear. The strengths and weaknesses of those approaches need to be assessed. Proposals in the fight against grade inflation (such as Princeton's proposal) need to be periodically assessed to document good practices in curbing grade problems.

Implications for Practice

Higher education administrators need to understand the complexity of college grading problems to be able to identify the right problems. This report, both conceptually and empirically, suggests that the increase in college grades exists; however, the underlying causes of grade increases are numerous. Some can be and should be resolved; others may be well beyond the control of higher education institutions. Policymakers and administrators need to focus on what they can do to improve college grading practices.

Changes in the characteristics of college students mirror overall shifts in the American population. These changes will continue to impact overall institutional GPAs but do not seem to have serious ramifications for the college grading process.

Grade inflation, either explicit or implicit, needs to be handled carefully. Explicit grade inflation is unethical and can negatively impact student motivation, learning, and involvement in academic activities. Implicit grade inflation can occur through the hiring of part-time faculty. Higher education administrators need to note the consequences of that shift. Changes in policies governing grading practices, such as treating withdrawals as nonpenalty grades, can have unwanted consequences on students' educational attainment and their future well-being (Adelman, 2004b). College and university administrators need to carefully rethink this subject.

Grading disparity deserves a more serious consideration by administrators and the faculty. It can potentially shortchange students' educational aspirations and generate undesirable competition among different academic units, causing grade inflation.

Faculty members, higher education administrators, and public policymakers alike are responsible for the well-being of colleges and universities as cherished social institutions in American society. They need to take steps to identify problems in college grading, to design strategies for prevention and correction so as to create an improved learning environment that promotes students' learning and personal development.

Diagnostic Method for Grading Problems

With a conceptual work delineating various grading problems and an extensive review of the empirical evidence, researchers now know that grade inflation cannot, by itself, reflect the complexity of grading problems in higher education. College grading problems include grade increase, grade inflation, grade compression, and grading disparity. Grade increase itself is not necessarily a problem, but it can serve as an early warning so that a deeper diagnosis can be made. Course grades, institutional GPAs, and institutional average GPAs are different indicators in unraveling grading problems. How can higher education leaders and administrators, then, diagnose whether or what types of grading problems might exist in their institutions? Is it possible for a college to develop an early warning system for potential grading problems?

It is a common practice for colleges and universities to acknowledge faculty who have served a long time. These faculty members might become assets in the effort to diagnose grading problems. Their reflection on their grading experiences and anecdotes could shed light on whether college grading practices have changed. Further, they may be able to explain trends if any changes have occurred. Frequent consultations with those faculty members could generate useful information about grading issues. One drawback might be that their recollections and reflections are nostalgic and possibly less accurate in reflecting the authentic history. But taken together, their insights might be reliable and prove valuable in improving campus practices.

Further, relatively large populations of career faculty members can offer a special opportunity to empirically examine grading problems on campus. One of the most sophisticated analyses of explicit grade inflation is to analyze grading patterns for the same faculty member teaching the same courses over time. Institutions can retrieve student course grades to perform empirical analyses that will shed light on grading problems (see, for example, a study by Jacobs, Johnson, and Keene, 1978). Analysis centered on student course grades can be further expanded to all faculty members so that implicit grade inflation can be examined to determine whether changes in faculty characteristics become a factor in explaining changes in students' grades in the same courses. Student course grades should be the unit of analysis to gain an accurate understanding of grade inflation. Meanwhile, a closer look at the relationship between student course grades and underlying meritorious measures (student academic ability reflected by the ACT, for example) in different time periods can answer questions about grade compression.

Grading disparity can be initially demonstrated by mapping out grades in different courses, major fields, and disciplines. More sophisticated analysis of grading disparity, however, needs to be accomplished through pair-wise comparisons of grades received by the same students in courses from different units. This treatment needs to be controlled for the confounding effects of individual characteristics for students who are enrolled in different courses or academic units. Of course, pair-wise comparisons of grades cannot eliminate the possibility that the match of student interests and course content (rather than grading standards) makes a difference in student course grades from different courses in different fields. In addition, longitudinal pair-wise comparisons of course grades can demonstrate whether the disparity in grading practices among different academic units is narrowing or widening over time.

In sum, grading problems are frustrating to higher education stakeholders. Research on grading problems can be challenging because of the complexity of the problem and the demand for quality data. This report is intended to reframe the problem and unravel the embedded complexity. It also explores solutions that can be adopted to deal with various grading problems. As the academy is searching for answers to the college grading problem, this report offers an opportunity to rethink the strategies in research, policy, and practice.

Appendix: Grading Proposals at Princeton University

Institutional Grading Limits

In undergraduate courses, A's (A+, A, A–) shall account for less than 35 percent of the grades given in any department or program in any given year.

In junior and senior independent work, A's (A+, A, A–) shall account for less than 55 percent of the grades given in any department in any given year.

Recognizing the responsibility of each faculty member to be cognizant of institutional grading limits, it shall be up to each department or program to determine how best to meet these limits. In so doing, the department or program shall take into account the range, size, and level of difficulty of undergraduate courses and the collective expectations of the faculty for independent work. The Faculty Committee on Examinations and Standing shall provide the faculty with models drawn from actual practice to illustrate how the grading limits might be met. It shall be the responsibility of the department chair or program director to lead faculty colleagues in adhering to these limits.

Reporting and Monitoring

Each fall, the Faculty Committee on Examinations and Standing shall report to the faculty on the grading record of the previous academic year.

The reports to the faculty shall document the grades they have actually given (that is, grades before P/D/F conversions are made).

All members of the faculty shall have access to grading data for all departments and programs, all divisions, and the University as a whole.

Each fall, the Faculty Committee on Examinations and Standing shall review the grading record of the previous year with a Select Committee on

Grading, whose membership shall include the Dean of the Faculty, the Dean of the College, the Registrar, and six members of the faculty (one department chair from each division, and two faculty members who have served previously on the Committee on Examinations and Standing). In the case of departments or programs that have not adhered to institutional grading limits, the Select Committee shall advise the Committee on Examinations and Standing on an appropriate strategy to assure adherence in the future.

The standard by which the grading record of a department or program will be evaluated will be the percentage of A's given over the previous three years.

Contextual Information

Information about each student's cumulative class standing at the end of the semester most recently completed shall be reported to the student on My Academic Record. That standing shall be reported in terms of quintiles—for example, first quintile, second quintile.

Grading Standards and Definitions

The Faculty Committee on Examinations and Standing shall publish and distribute to the faculty an expanded version of the Guide to Good Grading Practices that incorporates a number of examples of the grading standards adopted by the departments.

The Faculty Committee on Examinations and Standing shall undertake to redefine the meaning of each of the letter grades. This information shall be incorporated in the Undergraduate Announcement and, more briefly, on the back of the transcript.

Each year, the Dean of the College shall inform new members of the faculty about the University's grading expectations and policies and shall provide some historical background and context for the faculty's efforts to address grade inflation.

SOURCE: Princeton University, 2004.

References

Adelman, C. (1995a, May 17). A's aren't that easy. *New York Times,* A19.

Adelman, C. (1995b). *The new college course map of transcript files: Changes in course-taking and achievement, 1972–1993.* Washington, DC: Office of Educational Research and Improvement, U.S. Department of Education.

Adelman, C. (1996). Have you read your college transcript lately? *Change, 28*(1), 48–49.

Adelman, C. (1999a). *The new college course map of transcript files: Changes in course-taking and achievement, 1972–1993* (2nd ed.). Washington, DC: Office of Educational Research and Improvement, U.S. Department of Education.

Adelman, C. (1999b). The rest of the river. *University Business, 2*(1), 42–46, 48.

Adelman, C. (2001). Putting on the glitz: How tales from a few elite institutions form America's impression about higher education. *Connection, 15*(3), 24–31.

Adelman, C. (2004a). *The empirical curriculum: Changes in postsecondary course-taking, 1972–2000.* Washington, DC: Institute of Education Science, U.S. Department of Education.

Adelman, C. (2004b). *Principal indicators of student academic histories in postsecondary education: 1972–2000.* Washington, DC: Institute of Education Science, U.S. Department of Education.

Altbach, P. G., Berdahl, R. O., and Gumport, P. J. (Eds.). (1998). *American higher education in the twenty-first century: Social, political, and economic challenges.* Baltimore: Johns Hopkins University Press.

Altbach, P. G., Gumport, P. J., and Johnstone, D. B. (Eds.). (2001). *In defense of American higher education.* Baltimore: Johns Hopkins University Press.

Archibold, R. C. (1998, Feb. 18). Just because the grades are up, are Princeton students smarter? *New York Times,* A1.

Arenson, K. W. (2004, April 18). Is it grade inflation, or are students just smarter? *New York Times,* A1.

Astin, A. W. (1993). *Assessment for excellence: The philosophy and practice of assessment and evaluation in higher education.* Phoenix, AZ: American Council for Education and Oryx Press.

Astin, A. W. (1997). The changing American college student: Thirty year trends, 1966–1996. *Review of Higher Education, 21,* 115–135.

Bandura, A. (1986). *Social foundations of thought and action.* Englewood Cliffs, NJ: Prentice Hall.

Bandura, A. (1994). Self-efficacy. In V. S. Ramachaudran (Ed.), *Encyclopedia of human behavior* (Vol. 4, pp. 71–81). New York: Academic Press.

Bean, J. P. (1985). Interaction effects based on class level in an explanatory model of college student dropout syndrome. *American Educational Research Journal, 22,* 35–64.

Becker, G. S. (1965). A theory of the allocation of time. *Economic Journal, 75,* 493–517.

Becker, H. S. (1995). Introduction. In H. S. Becker, B. Geer, and E. C. Hughes, *Making the grade revisited.* New Brunswick, NJ: Transaction.

Becker, H. S., Geer, B., and Hughes, E. C. (1995). *Making the grade: The academic side of college life.* New Brunswick, NJ: Transaction.

Becker, W. E. (1982). The educational process and student achievement given uncertainty in measurement. *American Economic Review, 72,* 229–236.

Bejar, I. I., and Blew, E. O. (1981). Grade inflation and the validity of the scholastic aptitude test. *American Educational Research Journal, 18,* 143–156.

Betts, J. R., and Grogger, J. (2003). The impact of grading standards on student achievement, educational attainment, and entry-level earnings. *Economics of Education Review, 22,* 343–352.

Birnbaum, R. (1977). Factors related to university grade inflation. *Journal of Higher Education, 48,* 519–539.

Boesel, D., and Fredland, E. (1999). *College for all? Is there too much emphasis on getting a 4-year college degree?* Washington, DC: U.S. Department of Education.

Bowen, H. R. (1977). *Investment in learning.* San Francisco: Jossey-Bass.

Boyer, E. L. (1990). *Scholarship reconsidered: Priorities of the professoriate.* Princeton, NJ: Carnegie Foundation for the Advancement of Teaching.

Breland, H. M. (1976). *Grade inflation and declining SAT scores: A research viewpoint.* Paper presented at the annual meeting of the American Psychological Association, Sept. 3–7, Washington, DC. (ED 134 610)

Bressette, A. (2002). Arguments for plus/minus grading: A case study. *Educational Research Quarterly, 25*(3), 29–41.

Broski, M. S. (1998). *The cost and benefit of grades.* Unpublished doctoral dissertation. Fairfax, VA: George Mason University.

Centra, J. A. (2003). Will teachers receive higher student evaluations by giving higher grades and less coursework? *Research in Higher Education, 44,* 495–518.

Chen, S., and Cheng, D. (1999). *Remedial education and grading: A case study approach to two critical issues in American higher education.* Research report submitted to the Research Foundation of the City University of New York.

Chickering, A. W., and Reisser, L. (1993). *Education and identity* (2nd ed.). San Francisco: Jossey-Bass.

Chronicle of Higher Education. (2003). *Almanac 2003–4.* Washington, DC: The Chronicle of Higher Education.

Clark, B. R. (1983). *The higher education system: Academic organization in cross-national perspective.* Berkeley, CA: University of California Press.

Coleman, J., Hoffer, T., and Kilgore, S. (1982). *High school achievement: Catholic, public, and private schools compared.* New York: Basic Books.

Costrell, R. M. (1994). A simple model of educational standards. *American Economic Review, 84,* 956–971.

Cunningham, J. R., and Lawson, D. F. (1979). *The myth of the all-university GPA: An analysis of sources of apparent grade inflation.* Paper presented at the annual forum of the Association for Institutional Research, May 13–17, San Diego, CA. (ED 174 118)

de Nevers, N. (1984). An engineering solution to grade inflation. *Engineer Education, 74,* 661–663.

Dowd, A. C. (2000). Collegiate grading practices and the gender pay gap. *Education Policy Analysis Archive, 7*(30). Retrieved Jan. 13, 2003, from http://epaa.asu.edu/epaa/v8n10.html.

The Economist. (2002, March 9). An eye for an A. 74.

Edwards, C. H. (2000). Grade inflation: The effects on educational quality and personal well being. *Education, 120,* 538–547.

Eiszler, C. F. (2002). College students' evaluations of teaching and grade inflation. *Research in Higher Education, 43,* 483–501.

Ellenberg, J. (2002, Oct. 2). *Don't worry about grade inflation.* Retrieved Feb. 5, 2003, from http://slate.msn.com/id/2071759/.

Farkas, G., and Hotchkiss, L. (1989). Incentives and disincentives for subject matter difficulty and student effort: Course grade correlates across the stratification system. *Economics of Education Review, 8*(2), 121–132.

Figlio, D. N., and Lucas, M. E. (2000). *Do high grading standards affect student performance?* Cambridge, MA: National Bureau of Economic Research.

Flacks, R., and Thomas, S. (1998, Nov. 27). Among affluent students, a culture of disengagement. *Chronicle of Higher Education,* A48.

Fowler, F. C. (2000). *Policy studies for educational leaders: An introduction.* Upper Saddle River, NJ: Merrill.

Freeman, D. G. (1999). Grade divergence as a market outcome. *Journal of Economic Education, 30,* 344–351.

Frisbee, W. R. (1984). Course grades and academic performance by university students: A two-stage least-squares analysis. *Research in Higher Education, 20,* 345–365.

Gold, R. M., Reilly, A., Silberman, R., and Lehr, R. (1971). Academic achievement declines under pass-fail grading. *Journal of Experimental Education, 39,* 17–21.

Goldman, L. (1985). The betrayal of the gatekeepers: Grade inflation. *Journal of General Education, 37*(2), 97–121.

Goldman, R. D., and Hewitt, B. N. (1975). Adaptation-level as an explanation for differential standards in college grading. *Journal of Educational Measurement, 12,* 149–161.

Goldman, R. D., Schmidt, D. E., Hewitt, B. N., and Fisher, R. (1974). Grading practices in different major fields. *American Educational Research Journal, 11,* 343–357.

Goldman, R. D., and Slaughter, R. E. (1976). Why college grade point average is difficult to predict. *Journal of Educational Psychology, 68,* 9–14.

Goldman, R. D., and Widawski, M. A. (1976). A within-subjects technique for comparing college grading standards: Implications in validity of the evaluation of college achievement. *Educational and Psychological Measurement, 36,* 381–390.

Hanson, G. R. (1998). *Grade inflation: Myth or reality?* Retrieved June 18, 2004, from http://www.utexas.edu/student/research/reports/Inflation/Inflation.html.

Hanushek, E. (1979). Conceptual and empirical issues in the estimation of educational production function. *Journal of Human Resources, 14,* 351–388.

Hargis, C. H. (1990). *Grades and grading practices: Obstacles to improving education and to helping at-risk students.* Springfield, IL: Charles Thomas Publisher.

Healy, P. (2001, Oct. 7). Harvard's quiet secret: Rampant grade inflation. *The Boston Globe,* A1.

Heller, D. (Ed.). (2000). *The states and public higher education policy: Affordability, access, and accountability.* Baltimore: Johns Hopkins University Press.

Henry, G. T., and Rubenstein, R. (2002). Paying for grades: Impact of merit-based financial aid on educational quality. *Journal of Policy Analysis and Management, 21,* 93–109.

Herman, J. L., and Linn, R. L. (2003). Foreword. In *Accountability for educational quality: Shared responsibility* (p. 3). Washington, DC: American Educational Research Association.

Hoover, E. (2004, April 23). Princeton proposes limit on the number of A's. *Chronicle of Higher Education,* A40.

Horn, L., Peter, K., Rooney, K., and Malizio, A. G. (2002). *Profile of undergraduates in U.S. postsecondary educational institutions: 1999–2000.* Washington, DC: Office of Educational Research and Improvement, U.S. Department of Education.

Hu, S. (2003). *Grade inflation in higher education: A critical review and synthesis.* Paper presented at the annual meeting of the American Educational Research Association, April 21–25, Chicago, IL.

Hu, S., and Kuh, G. D. (1998). *Unraveling the complexity of the increase of college grades from the mid-1980s to the mid-1990s.* Paper presented at the annual meeting of Association for the Study of Higher Education, Nov. 5–8, Miami, FL.

Hu, S., and Kuh, G. D. (2003). Maximizing what students get out of college: Testing a learning productivity model. *Journal of College Student Development, 44,* 185–203.

Indiana University Office of the Registrar. (2004). *The expanded context transcript.* Retrieved June 18, 2004, from http://www.indiana.edu/~registra/Services/contexttranscript.html.

Jacobs, L. C., Johnson, J. J., and Keene, J. M. (1978). *University grade inflation after controlling for courses and academic ability.* Bloomington, IN: Bureau of Evaluative Studies and Testing, Indiana University. (ED 156 050)

Johnson, V. E. (1997). An alternative to traditional GPA in evaluating student performance. *Statistical Science, 12,* 257–278.

Johnson, V. E. (2003). *Grade inflation: A crisis in college education.* New York: Springer Verlag.

Juola, A. E. (1976). *Grade inflation in higher education: What can or should we do?* Paper presented at the annual meeting of the National Council on Measurement in Education, April 19–23, San Francisco. (ED 129 917)

Juola, A. E. (1980). *Grade inflation in higher education—1979. Is it over?* East Lansing, MI: Learning and Evaluation Services, Michigan State University. (ED 189 129)

Kamber, R., and Biggs, M. (2002, April 12). Grade conflation: A question of credibility. *Chronicle of Higher Education,* B14.

Karlins, M., Kaplan, M., and Stuart, W. (1969). Academic attitudes and performance as a function of differential grading systems. *Journal of Experimental Education, 37,* 38–50.

Kezar, A. (2004). Obtaining integrity? Reviewing and examining the charter between higher education and society. *Review of Higher Education, 27,* 429–459.

Kohn, A. (1992). *No contest: The case against competition.* Boston: Houghton Mifflin.

Kohn, A. (2002, Nov. 8). The dangerous myth of grade inflation. *Chronicle of Higher Education,* B7.

Koretz, D., and Berends, M. (2001). *Changes in high school grading standards in mathematics, 1982–1992.* Retrieved Jan. 14, 2003, from http://www.rand.org/publications/MR/MR1445/.

Krathwohl, D. R. (1997). *Methods of educational and social science research: An integrated approach.* New York: Longman.

Krautmann, A. C., and Sander, W. (1999). Grades and student evaluation of teachers. *Economics of Education Review, 18,* 59–63.

Kuh, G. D. (1999). How are we doing? Tracking the quality of the undergraduate experience— 1960s to the present. *Review of Higher Education 22,* 99–120.

Kuh, G. D. (2003). What we're learning about student engagement from NSSE. *Change, 35*(2), 24–32.

Kuh, G. D., and Hu, S. (1999). Unraveling the complexity of the increase in college grades from the mid-1980s to the mid-1990s. *Educational Evaluation and Policy Analysis, 21,* 297–320.

Kuh, G. D., Hu, S., and Vesper, N. (2000). They shall be known by what they do: An activities-based typology of college students. *Journal of College Student Development, 41,* 228–244.

Kuh, G. D., Schuh, J. H., Whitt, E. J., and Associates. (1991). *Involving colleges: Successful approaches to fostering student learning and personal development outside the classroom.* San Francisco: Jossey-Bass.

Lavin, D. E. (1965). *The prediction of academic performance: A theoretical analysis and review of research.* New York: Russell Sage Foundation.

Levine, A., and Cureton, J. S. (1998). *When hope and fear collide: A portrait of today's college student.* San Francisco: Jossey-Bass.

Mansfield, H. C. (2001, April 6). Grade inflation: It's time to face the facts. *Chronicle of Higher Education,* B24.

Marsh, H. W., and Roche, L. A. (2000). Effects of grading leniency and low workload on students' evaluations of teaching: Popular myth, bias, validity, or innocent bystanders? *Journal of Educational Psychology, 92,* 202–228.

McDonnell, L. M. (1994). Assessment policy as persuasion and regulation. *American Journal of Education, 102,* 391–420.

McDonnell, L. M., and Elmore, R. F. (1987). Getting the job done: Alternative policy instruments. *Educational Evaluation and Policy Analysis, 9,* 133–152.

McKeachie, W. J., and others. (1990). *Teaching and learning in the college classroom: A review of the research literature* (2nd ed.). Ann Arbor: University of Michigan.

McSpirit, S., and Jones, K. E. (1999, Sept. 20). Grade inflation rates among different ability students, controlling for other factors. *Education Policy Analysis Archive, 7*(30). Retrieved Jan. 13, 2003, from http://epaa.asu.edu/epaa/v7n30.html.

Miller, R. H. (1965). Students show a preparation increase but no increase in grades was shown. *College and University, 41,* 28–30.

Millman, J., Slovacek, S. P., Kulick, E., and Mitchell, K. J. (1983). Does grade inflation affect the reliability of grades? *Research in Higher Education, 19,* 423–429.

Milton, O., Pollio, H. R., and Eison, J. A. (1986). *Making sense of college grades.* San Francisco: Jossey-Bass.

Mitchell, L. C. (1998, May 8). Inflation isn't the only thing wrong with grading. *Chronicle of Higher Education,* A72.

Moore, M., and Trahan, R. (1998). Tenure status and grading practices. *Sociological Perspectives, 41,* 775–781.

Mortenson, T. G. (1997, Feb.). Georgia's HOPE Scholarship program: Good intentions, strong funding, bad design. *Postsecondary Education Opportunity Newsletter, 56.*

Mullen, R. (1995). *Indicators of grade inflation.* Paper presented at the annual forum of the Association for Institutional Research, May 28–31, Boston, MA.

Nagle, B. (1998). A proposal for dealing with grade inflation: The relative performance index. *Journal of Education for Business, 74*(1), 40–44.

National Center for Public Policy and Higher Education. (2001). *Measuring up 2000.* San Jose, CA: National Center for Public Policy and Higher Education.

National Center for Public Policy and Higher Education. (2002). *Measuring up 2002.* San Jose, CA: National Center for Public Policy and Higher Education.

National Center for Public Policy and Higher Education. (2004). *Measuring up 2004.* San Jose, CA: National Center for Public Policy and Higher Education.

Naughton, B. A., Suen, A. Y., and Shavelson, R. J. (2003). *Accountable for what? Understanding the learning objectives in state higher education accountability programs.* Paper presented at the annual meeting of the American Educational Research Association, April 21–25, Chicago, IL.

Olsen, D. R. (1997). *Grade inflation: Reality or myth? Student preparation level vs. grades at Brigham Young University, 1975–1994.* Paper presented at the annual forum of the Association for Institutional Research, May 18–21, Orlando, FL.

Pascarella, E. T., and Terenzini, P. T. (1991). *How college affects students: Findings and insights from twenty years of research.* San Francisco: Jossey-Bass.

Paulsen, M. B., and Smart, J. C. (Eds.). (2002). *The finance of higher education: Theory, research, policy, and practice.* New York: Agathon.

Pedersen, D. (1997, March 3). When an A is average. *Newsweek,* 64.

Prather, J. E., Smith, G., and Kodras, J. E. (1979). A longitudinal study of grades in 144 undergraduate courses. *Research in Higher Education, 10,* 11–24.

Princeton University. (2004). *Report to faculty on grading proposals.* Retrieved June 18, 2004, from http://www.princeton.edu/~odoc/grading_proposals/index.html.

Pugh, R. G. (2000). The expanded grade context record at Indiana University and its relationship to grade inflation. *College and University, 75*(4), 3–12.

Rau, W., and Durand, A. (2000). The academic ethic and college grades: Does hard work help students to "make the grade"? *Sociology of Education, 73,* 19–38.

Robbins, S. B., and others. (2004). Do psychosocial and study skill factors predict college outcomes? A meta-analysis. *Psychological Bulletin, 130,* 261–288.

Rojstaczer, S. (2003). *Grade inflation at American colleges and universities.* Retrieved Feb. 4, 2004, from http://www.gradeinflation.com/.

Rosovsky, H., and Hartley, M. (2002). *Evaluation and the academy: Are we doing the right thing? Grade inflation and letters of recommendation.* Cambridge, MA: American Academy of Arts and Sciences.

Sabot, R., and Wakeman-Linn, J. (1991). Grade inflation and course choice. *Journal of Economic Perspectives, 5*(1), 159–171.

Schuman, H. (2001). Students' effort and reward in college settings. *Sociology of Education, 74,* 73–77.

Schuman, H., Walsh, E., Olson, C., and Etheridge, B. (1985). Effort and reward: The assumption that college grades are affected by quantity of study. *Social Forces, 63,* 945–966.

Schuster, J., and Finkelstein, M. (forthcoming). *The American faculty.* Baltimore: Johns Hopkins University Press.

Shavelson, R. J., and Huang, L. (2003). Responding responsibly to the frenzy to assess learning in higher education. *Change, 35*(1), 11–19.

Shea, C. (1994, Jan. 5). The subtleties of grade inflation. *Chronicle of Higher Education,* A45–A46.

Shoichet, C. E. (2002, July 12). Reports of grade inflation may be inflated. *Chronicle of Higher Education,* A37.

Singleton, R. (1978). Effects of grade inflation on satisfaction with final grade: A case of relative deprivation. *Journal of Social Psychology, 105*(1), 37–42.

Singleton, R., and Smith, E. R. (1978). Does grade inflation decrease the reliability of grades? *Journal of Educational Measurement, 15*(1), 37–41.

Slavin, R. E. (2002). Evidence-based education policies: Transforming educational practice and research. *Educational Researcher, 31*(7), 15–21.

Sloop, S. L. (2000). *Keep a B and go to college free: An examination of grade inflation.* Unpublished doctoral dissertation. Athens: University of Georgia.

Sonner, B. S. (2000). A is for "adjunct": Examining grade inflation in higher education. *Journal of Education for Business, 76*(1), 5–9.

Stone, J. E. (1995). Inflated grades, inflated enrollment, and inflated budgets: An analysis and call for review at the state level. *Education Policy Analysis Archives, 3*(11). Retrieved Jan. 13, 2003, from http://epaa.asu.edu/epaa/v3n11.html.

Suslow, S. (1977). Grade inflation: End of a trend? *Change, 9*(3), 44–45.

Van-Laar, C., Sidanius, J., Rabinowitz, J. L., and Sinclair, S. (1999). The three Rs of academic achievement: Reading, writing, and racism. *Personality and Social Psychology Bulletin, 25,* 139–151.

Volkwein, J. F., and others. (2000). *A multi-campus study of academic performance and cognitive growth among native freshman, two-year transfers, and four-year transfers.* Paper presented at the annual forum of the Association for Institutional Research, May 21–23, Cincinnati, OH.

Von Wittich, C. (1972). The impact of the pass-fail system upon achievement of college students. *Journal of Higher Education, 43,* 499–508.

Walvoord, B. F., and Anderson, V. J. (1998). *Effective grading.* San Francisco: Jossey-Bass.

Webb, S. C. (1959). Measured changes in college grading standards. *College Board Review, 39,* 27–30.

Wegman, J. R. (1987). An economic analysis of grade inflation using indexing. *College and University, 62*(2), 137–146.

Willingham, W. W., Lewis, C., Morgan, R., and Ramist, L. (1990). *Predicting college grades: An analysis of institutional trends over two decades.* New York: College Board and Educational Testing Service.

Wingspread Group on Higher Education. (1993). *An American imperative: Higher expectations for higher education.* Racine, WI: The Johnson Foundation.

Wood, A. L., Ridley, D. R., and Summerville, R. M. (1999). *University grade inflation through twenty years: An analytical and empirical investigation.* Paper presented at the annual meeting of the Association for the Study of Higher Education, Nov. 18–21, San Antonio, TX. (ED 439 646)

Young, J. R. (2002, Dec. 6). Homework? What homework? *Chronicle of Higher Education,* A35–A37.

Name Index

A

Adelman, C., 2, 4, 6, 7, 11, 14, 16, 30, 31, 32, 39, 51, 53, 78

Altbach, P. G., 5

Anderson, V. J., 5, 10, 23, 68, 69, 76

Angelo, 5

Archibold, R. C., 1

Arenson, K. W., 1

Astin, A. W., 15, 42, 50

B

Bean, J. P., 53, 59

Becker, G. S., 10

Becker, H. S., 37, 59

Becker, W. E., 25, 26, 38

Bejar, I. I., 34, 37

Berdahl, R. O., 5

Berends, M., 16

Betts, J. R., 25

Biggs, M., 24, 63, 64

Birnbaum, R., 1, 9, 15, 16, 18, 45

Blew, E. O., 34, 37

Bnadura, A., 10

Boesel, D., 48, 50

Bowen, H. R., 26

Boyer, E. L., 60, 61

Breland, H. M., 37

Bressette, A., 65

Broski, M. S., 54, 58, 66

C

Centra, J. A., 55, 56, 57

Chen, S., 9, 12, 13

Cheng, D., 9, 12, 13

Chickering, A. W., 50

Clark, B. R., 10

Coleman, J., 10

Costrell, R. M., 25

Cunningham, J. R., 20

Cureton, J. S., 1, 15, 30, 39

D

de Nevers, N., 65

Dowd, A. C., 26

Durand, A., 12

E

Edwards, C. H., 23

Eison, J. A., 5, 59

Eiszler, C. F., 55, 56, 57

Ellenberg, J., 37

Elmore, R. F., 68, 69

Etheridge, B., 12

F

Farkas, G., 10, 12

Fisher, R., 54

Flacks, R., 50

Fowler, F. C., 22, 68

Fredland, E., 48, 50

Freeman, D. G., 54

Frisbee, W. R., 12

G

Geer, B., 59

Gold, R. M., 25, 39

Prather, J. E., 20, 35, 50
Pugh, R. G., 64

R

Rabinowitz, J. L., 10, 12
Ramist, L., 13
Rau, W., 12
Reilly, A., 25
Reisser, L., 50
Ridley, D. R., 10, 14, 33
Robbins, S. B., 12
Roche, L. A., 10, 55
Rojstaczer, S., 1, 2, 30
Rooney, K., 2, 32, 39
Rosovsky, H., 1, 2, 18, 36, 45, 58, 64, 65, 67
Rubenstein, R., 59

S

Sabot, R., 26, 38, 53, 55
Sander, W., 56
Schmidt, D. E., 54
Schuh, J. H., 50
Schuman, H., 12
Shavelson, R. J., 4, 10, 26
Shea, C., 55
Sidanius, J., 10, 12
Silberman, R., 25
Sinclair, S., 10, 12
Singleton, R., 25, 37
Slaughter, R. E., 20
Slovacek, S. P., 37
Smart, J. C., 5

Smith, E. R., 37
Smith, G., 20, 35, 50
Sonner, B. S., 13
Stone, J. E., 54
Stuart, W., 25
Suen, A. Y., 4, 26
Summerville, R. M., 10, 14, 33
Suslow, S., 31

T

Terenzini, P. T., 14, 50, 59
Thomas, S., 50
Trahan, R., 13

V

Van-Laar, C., 10, 12
Vesper, N., 50
Volkwein, J. F., 11, 12, 14
Von Wittich, C., 25

W

Wakeman-Linn, J., 26, 38, 53, 55
Walsh, E., 12
Walvoord, B. F., 5, 10, 23, 68, 69, 76
Webb, S. C., 29
Wegman, J. R., 15, 24
Whitt, E. J., 50
Widawski, M. A., 20, 39
Willingham, W. W., 13
Wood, A. L., 10, 14, 33

Y

Young, J. R., 50

Subject Index

About the Author

Shouping Hu is associate professor of higher education in the Department of Educational Leadership and Policy Studies at Florida State University. He earned a B.S. in geography and had two years of graduate study in higher education at Peking University. He completed an M.A. in economics and a Ph.D. in higher education at Indiana University. His current research focuses on postsecondary participation, college student learning, and higher education policy.

About the ASHE-ERIC
Higher Education Reports Series

Since 1983, the ASHE (formerly ASHE-ERIC) Higher Education Report Series has been providing researchers, scholars, and practitioners with timely and substantive information on the critical issues facing higher education. Each monograph presents a definitive analysis of a higher education problem or issue, based on a thorough synthesis of significant literature and institutional experiences. Topics range from planning to diversity and multiculturalism, to performance indicators, to curricular innovations. The mission of the Series is to link the best of higher education research and practice to inform decision making and policy. The reports connect conventional wisdom with research and are designed to help busy individuals keep up with the higher education literature. Authors are scholars and practitioners in the academic community. Each report includes an executive summary, review of the pertinent literature, descriptions of effective educational practices, and a summary of key issues to keep in mind to improve educational policies and practice.

The Series is one of the most peer reviewed in higher education. A National Advisory Board made up of ASHE members reviews proposals. A National Review Board of ASHE scholars and practitioners reviews completed manuscripts. Six monographs are published each year and they are approximately 120 pages in length. The reports are widely disseminated through Jossey-Bass and John Wiley & Sons, and they are available online to subscribing institutions through Wiley InterScience (http://www.interscience.wiley.com).

Call for Proposals

The ASHE Higher Education Report Series is actively looking for proposals. We encourage you to contact one of the editors, Dr. Kelly Ward (kaward@wsu.edu) or Dr. Lisa Wolf-Wendel (lwolf@ku.edu), with your ideas.

Recent Titles

Back Issue/Subscription Order Form

Copy or detach and send to:

Jossey-Bass, A Wiley Imprint, 989 Market Street, San Francisco CA 94103-1741

Call or fax toll-free: Phone 888-378-2537 6:30AM – 3PM PST; Fax 888-481-2665

Back Issues: Please send me the following issues at $24 each
(Important: please include series abbreviation and issue number.
For example AEHE 28:1)

_____

_____

_____

$ _____   Total for single issues

$ _____   SHIPPING CHARGES: SURFACE   Domestic Canadian
First Item $5.00 $6.00
Each Add'l Item $3.00 $1.50
For next-day and second-day delivery rates, call the number listed above

Subscriptions   Please ❑ start ❑ renew my subscription to *ASHE-ERIC Higher Education Reports* for the year 2_____at the following rate:

U.S.	❑ Individual $165	❑ Institutional $175
Canada	❑ Individual $165	❑ Institutional $235
All Others	❑ Individual $213	❑ Institutional $286

❑ Online subscriptions available too!

**For more information about online subscriptions visit
www.interscience.wiley.com**

$ _____   Total single issues and subscriptions (Add appropriate sales tax for your state for single issue orders. No sales tax for U.S. subscriptions. Canadian residents, add GST for subscriptions and single issues.)

❑Payment enclosed (U.S. check or money order only)

❑VISA ❑ MC ❑ AmEx ❑ #_____ Exp. Date _____

Signature _____ Day Phone _____
❑ Bill Me (U.S. institutional orders only. Purchase order required.)

Purchase order # _____
Federal Tax ID13559302   GST 89102 8052

Name _____

Address _____

_____

Phone _____ E-mail _____

For more information about Jossey-Bass, visit our Web site at **www.josseybass.com**

ASHE-ERIC HIGHER EDUCATION REPORT
IS NOW AVAILABLE ONLINE AT WILEY INTERSCIENCE

What is Wiley InterScience?

Wiley InterScience is the dynamic online content service from John Wiley & Sons delivering the full text of over 300 leading scientific, technical, medical, and professional journals, plus major reference works, the acclaimed Current Protocols laboratory manuals, and even the full text of select Wiley print books online.

What are some special features of Wiley InterScience?

Wiley Interscience Alerts is a service that delivers table of contents via e-mail for any journal available on Wiley InterScience as soon as a new issue is published online.
Early View is Wiley's exclusive service presenting individual articles online as soon as they are ready, even before the release of the compiled print issue. These articles are complete, peer-reviewed, and citable.
CrossRef is the innovative multi-publisher reference linking system enabling readers to move seamlessly from a reference in a journal article to the cited publication, typically located on a different server and published by a different publisher.

How can I access Wiley InterScience?

Visit http://www.interscience.wiley.com.

Guest Users can browse Wiley InterScience for unrestricted access to journal Tables of Contents and Article Abstracts, or use the powerful search engine.
Registered Users are provided with a *Personal Home Page* to store and manage customized alerts, searches, and links to favorite journals and articles. Additionally, Registered Users can view free Online Sample Issues and preview selected material from major reference works.
Licensed Customers are entitled to access full-text journal articles in PDF, with select journals also offering full-text HTML.

How do I become an Authorized User?

Authorized Users are individuals authorized by a paying Customer to have access to the journals in Wiley InterScience. For example, a University that subscribes to Wiley journals is considered to be the Customer.
Faculty, staff and students authorized by the University to have access to those journals in Wiley InterScience are Authorized Users. Users should contact their Library for information on which Wiley journals they have access to in Wiley InterScience.

ASK YOUR INSTITUTION ABOUT WILEY INTERSCIENCE TODAY!